100

T0046468

THINGS TO DO IN
CINCINNATI
BEFORE YOU
DIE

Roebling Suspension Bridge
Courtesy of Cincinnati Story Project

100

3rd Edition

THINGS TO DO IN
CINCINNATI
BEFORE YOU
DIE

• •

RICK PENDER

REEDY PRESS

Permissions may be sought directly from Reedy Press at the above mailing address or via our website at www.reedypress.com.

Library of Congress Control Number: 2023930172

ISBN: 9781681064475

Design by Jill Halpin

All photos are by the author unless otherwise noted.

Printed in the United States of America
23 24 25 26 27   5 4 3 2 1

We (the publisher and the author) have done our best to provide the most accurate information available when this book was completed. However, we make no warranty, guarantee, or promise about the accuracy, completeness, or currency of the information provided, and we expressly disclaim all warranties, express or implied. Please note that attractions, company names, addresses, websites, and phone numbers are subject to change or closure, and this is outside of our control. We are not responsible for any loss, damage, injury, or inconvenience that may occur due to the use of this book. When exploring new destinations, please do your homework before you go. You are responsible for your own safety and health when using this book.

DEDICATION

To my wife Joan, who inspires me—and many others—to say
good things about Cincinnati every day. And to our English
bulldog Bella, who keeps my feet warm while I'm writing.

• •

CONTENTS

• •

Music and Entertainment

• •

Sports and Recreation

Culture and History

• •

• •

• •

PREFACE

It was easy to come up with "100 things to do" in Cincinnati when I wrote the first edition of this book in 2016. In fact, I had to trim my list, which was nearly twice that long. My second edition, published in late 2019, was about 20 percent new, but the pandemic changed things even more, so this new third edition was needed. More than a third of the material is new or revised.

My goal is to offer a satisfying cross-section of things that are unique to the "Queen City of the West." When poet Henry Wadsworth Longfellow gave Cincinnati that appellation back in the 19th century, the city was truly on America's western frontier, the last stop before leaving civilization behind and heading off to parts unknown. That's no longer the case, but it still has a kind of royalty to it.

I wasn't born and raised in Cincinnati. But I've lived and worked here most of my adult life and have now retired here. I love giving tours and hearing people say, "I had no idea this was such an interesting and picturesque place." Many visitors come with low expectations, imagining Cincinnati to be a "fly-over" city in the flat, boring Midwest. Thanks to the Ohio River, we have hills and valleys and overlooks. Our steep hillsides remind people of San Francisco, and the scenery here is far from boring. With history and professional sports, arts and culture, a restaurant scene that's the rival of any city, and more craft breweries than you can shake a stein at, Cincinnati continues to be an exciting place to explore and to call home.

I hope this new edition of my book inspires you to check out as many of Cincinnati's unique attractions as possible—two a week will keep you busy for most of a year! And you'll encounter the hospitable people who call the towns and neighborhoods in Ohio and Kentucky home—and be glad to have met them.

A few notes: The City of Cincinnati is the heart of this region, but our metropolitan area covers an area much vaster than that one municipality. In fact, "Greater Cincinnati" is a tri-state region, encompassing four counties in Ohio, two in Indiana, and three in Northern Kentucky. Unique offerings and destinations are to be found in all directions, and this book will point you to lots of them. But along the way, I bet you'll discover some more, so don't hesitate to send me your finds: pender.rick@gmail.com. I'll share your recommendations via my Rick Pender Writes group page on Facebook.

When you go exploring, I recommend calling ahead or checking online (phone numbers and websites are listed with most entries) to be sure you have up-to-date information about your destination. Everything was accurate when I researched these recommendations, but life does go on and things do change. That's why a third edition was necessary!

Have fun!

Rick Pender

ACKNOWLEDGMENTS

Just as I did with the first edition of this book, I relied on the insights of many friends who know things about Cincinnati that I had yet to learn. Past assistance from Bob and new ideas from Kareem helped me ensure that Northern Kentucky got its share of "things to do." Jerri and Lyn's suggestions continued to be helpful about arts and culture, with a meaningful dollop of shopping, and I picked Debba's brain for a few more. My "Game Night" friends know how to have a good time, and some of their ideas show up this time. Venus, a longtime travel advisor who has moved to the urban core, was another fine source of great things to do around town.

Arnold's Bar & Grill

FOOD
AND DRINK

HAVE A THREE-WAY
IN A CINCINNATI CHILI PARLOR

Say what? This is not an indecent proposal! Cincinnati chili is unlike any chili you've tried elsewhere. A popular item of local cuisine, it's actually finely ground beef spiced with tomato paste, cinnamon, cloves, allspice, and a dash of chocolate ladled over spaghetti or a hot dog and topped with grated cheddar cheese. Cincinnatians crave it and seek it out at hundreds of "chili parlors" all over town.

Local purveyors include:
Skyline Chili (130 parlors around town)
skylinechili.com

Gold Star (93 locations)
goldstarchili.com

Dixie Chili (locations in Newport, Erlanger, and Covington, KY)
dixiechili.com

Camp Washington Chili
3005 Colerain Ave., 513-541-0061
campwashingtonchili.com

Price Hill Chili
4920 Glenway Ave., 513-471-9507
pricehillchili.com

Blue Ash Chili
9565 Kenwood Rd., 513-984-6107
blueashchili.com

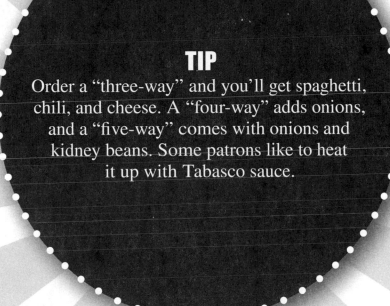

TIP

Order a "three-way" and you'll get spaghetti, chili, and cheese. A "four-way" adds onions, and a "five-way" comes with onions and kidney beans. Some patrons like to heat it up with Tabasco sauce.

BELLY UP
TO CINCINNATI'S OLDEST BAR

Since Simon Arnold opened his tavern in 1861, this Downtown watering hole has been a destination—and in continuous operation—longer than any other bar in the city. Arnold's Bar & Grill occupies two historic buildings: a one-time barbershop, which is today's bar with lots of local brews, and a feed store with a stable, transformed into a popular year-round courtyard where musicians perform on Friday and Saturday nights. Head up to the second floor to see the bathtub used to make gin in-house. Arnold's has an eclectic menu, too, featuring Greek spaghetti (feta cheese, olives, and garlic sauce over linguini), a popular item since 1957.

210 E 8th St., 513-421-6234
arnoldsbarandgrill.com

TIP
Show up on election night and you're likely to find more than one local politician celebrating a win or mourning a loss in the courtyard.

GET SOME GOETTA

When immigrants from northwestern Germany arrived in Cincinnati in the 19th century, they brought along a peasant dish made from ground meat (usually pork and beef) mixed with steel-cut (pinhead) oats and spices, formed into a loaf, sliced and fried in two-inch squares, and usually served for breakfast. They called it goetta (GET-uh), and today it's a popular—even kind of hip—local food item, even if you're not a German peasant. Glier's Meats produces more than a million pounds of it annually, most of which is sold locally.

533 Goetta Pl., Covington, KY, 859-291-1800
goetta.com

TIP

You can celebrate at Glier's Goettafest every August on the Ohio riverfront in Newport, Kentucky. The festival features many creative applications of goetta: burgers, egg rolls, pizza, lasagna, burritos, Reuben sandwiches, and more (goettafest.com). If one festival isn't enough, there's another one every June at Mainstrasse Village in Covington, Kentucky.

mainstrasse.org

SAMPLE "FRENCH POT" ICE CREAM
AT GRAETER'S

Since 1870, the Graeter family has made thick, rich, "irresistible" ice cream using a small-batch process that maintains high quality in two-gallon batches. Half of its 20 or so year-round flavors use the best irregular dark chocolate chips you've ever tasted. Their products have been called "the best ice cream in the world," and fans include Oprah Winfrey and Harry Connick Jr. It's sold in pint containers in grocery stores, but the best experience is to get a scoop in a sugar cone at one of Graeter's two dozen or so parlors across Southwest Ohio and Northern Kentucky. (Check out the baked goods and candy too.)

Many locations
Corporate Office: 1175 Regina Graeter Way, 800-721-3323
graeters.com

TIP

Graeter's will ship ice cream nationally, packed in coolers with dry ice. Do it once or twice and your out-of-town friends will start showing up unexpectedly!

graeters.com

TAKE A SEAT
AT THE BAKER'S TABLE

In 2019, this Newport farm-to-table restaurant and bar that capitalizes on excellent bread baking was recognized by *Eater* as one of the 16 best new restaurants in the United States. It had already come in fourth on *USA Today*'s list of "Best New Restaurants in America." It's a place where complex menu items are made into something you'll never forget, and it's done with simple approaches. The risotto has been repeatedly cited, pulling together oyster mushrooms, ramps, and asparagus—but even simple fare like a grilled cheese on sourdough is memorable. And finish off with a salted chocolate chip cookie. The owners also operate The Baker's Table Bakery across the street, a fine stop for bread, pastries, and espresso in the daytime and for farm-to-table pizza and natural wines in the evening.

The Baker's Table
1004 Monmouth St., Newport, KY, 859-261-1941

Baker's Table Bakery
1001 Monmouth St., Newport, KY

bakerstablenewport.com

LINE UP FOR BARBECUE
AT ELI'S

You can find good barbecue at more than one place in Cincinnati, but serious connoisseurs keep coming back to Eli's BBQ's two locations, in the East End and near Findlay Market. It's the go-to-joint for pulled pork and smoked turkey (as well as all-beef franks), but the top of the line are hickory smoked ribs in choices from two bones to a dozen—or just the tips, if you prefer. Everything is surprisingly affordable, so you'll probably want to stock up on sides while you're at it—from mac and cheese, Southern coleslaw, and baked beans to mashed potatoes and jalapeno cheddar grits. Eli's will cater office events, family gatherings, weddings, and more with its great service and easy locations.

3313 Riverside Dr. (East End)
133 W Elder St. (near Findlay Market)
3715 Madison Rd. (Oakley)
13900 Montgomery Rd. (Montgomery)
elisbarbeque.com

DINE IN A HALLOWED (RESTAURANT) SPACE
AT BOCA

For more than four decades, the Maisonette was the go-to destination for Cincinnati connoisseurs, earning 41 consecutive five-star ratings from Mobil Travel Guide. But it closed in 2005, and the space remained vacant until David Falk, who spent two years there as a young chef early in his career, moved in. It's now Boca, an extravagantly renovated and gloriously redecorated downtown home for fine dining. Falk converted the one-time downstairs chophouse into Sotto, a delightful, casual trattoria, featuring handmade pasta. But Boca is the showplace, described by Falk as "part *La Bohème*, part *Beauty and the Beast*," featuring eclectic, elegant fare that's hard to categorize—a touch of Italian with a dose of continental cuisine but including Amish Chicken, Peking Duck, and a signature favorite: caramelized Brussels sprouts. It's the most memorable dining experience in Cincinnati.

Boca
114 E 6th St., 513-977-6886
bocacincinnati.com

Sotto
118 E 6th St., 513-542-2022
sottocincinnati.com

ENJOY WEST SIDE FINE DINING
AT IVORY HOUSE

Cincinnati's West Side has not traditionally been known for upscale dining—but Ivory House has changed that. Situated in the historic Westwood Town Hall district, its motto is "Familiar Food, Elevated," and that means carefully made, nostalgic steakhouse and seafood classics are enhanced with special, inventive touches. Even items like potato salad are way above average, and there are small plates including mussels diablo, shrimp and grits, and ham and bean agnolotti. The restaurant's name refers to James N. Gamble, son of the founder of Procter & Gamble who invented Ivory Soap. He was also the last person to serve as Westwood's mayor before it became a city neighborhood. The "ivory" theme is carried out by a white grand piano and decorative touches in the black-grey-white range. It's a great place for Sunday brunch, and the extensive wine menu has a wide range of choices. Thanks to its proximity to nearby West Side Brewing, diners can enjoy Ivory House Amber, as well as bottled and canned brews. It's popular with West Siders, but more and more customers are coming from all points on the compass.

2998 Harrison Ave., Westwood, 513-389-0175
ivoryhousecincy.com

WHERE'S THE BEEF IN CINCINNATI?
IT'S AT JEFF RUBY'S STEAKHOUSE

For several decades Jeff Ruby has been known as both a showman and a restaurateur, serving high-end steaks in plush settings to carnivorous Cincinnatians. In 2022, his showy iconic steakhouse moved a few blocks south to the very heart of downtown, on Vine Street, adjacent to Fountain Square. At the valet stand is an oversize bronze replica of the iconic Wall Street bull. It's his largest and most luxurious venue yet, which is saying something in the context of Ruby's other eateries, The Precinct in Columbia-Tusculum and Carlo & Johnny in Montgomery. The new space replicates the classic Art Deco opulence that was the trademark at the previous location, and the emphasis on lively entertainment featuring a mother-of-pearl and gold-plated 1865 Steinway baby grand piano is still top-notch. The service team is a point of pride: Ruby says, "Our food fills our guests' stomachs, but our people fill their hearts." It's a top-dollar stop, but it's a Cincinnati favorite for celebrities and sports stars.

Jeff Ruby's Steakhouse
505 Vine St., 513-784-1200

The Precinct
311 Delta Ave., 513-321-5454

Carlo & Johnny
9769 Montgomery Rd., 513-936-8600

jeffruby.com

GET SOME CAJUN FARE
AT KNOTTY PINE ON THE BAYOU

You don't have to travel all the way to Louisiana. This friendly roadhouse is the only place in Greater Cincinnati to find genuine savory Louisiana homestyle fare, the next best thing to a visit to New Orleans. Try fried catfish fillets or garlic sauteed shrimp. From February to May, crawfish is the feature: serious diners flock there for the crawfish etouffée. Guests keep coming back for the year-round gumbo packed with andouille sausage, chicken, and vegetables. Try it once and you'll likely become a regular. If you can't decide, order up a Cajun sampler with blackened chicken and filet tips, sauteed shrimp, a cup of gumbo, and another of red beans and rice.

6302 Licking Pike, Cold Spring, KY, 859-781-2200
theknottypineonthebayou.com

SAMPLE
FINE RESTAURANTS
ON COVINGTON'S MAINSTRASSE

Downtown Covington has lots of great dining spots to choose from. Coppin's, within the historic Covington Hotel, has beer and wine, but especially a nice array of Kentucky bourbon. Meat (cured at Kenny's Farmhouse) and cheese (from Urban Stead) keep the local flavors that repeat diners appreciate. Frida's 602, with décor inspired by Mexican artist Frida Kahlo, is the place for varied tacos, margaritas, and mezcal while the focus is on tasty and simple Mexican fare and a few Cuban items. Across Main St. (and by the same owner) is Otto's, with a varied menu that includes tomato pie, shrimp and grits, short ribs—comfort food extraordinaire. Next door to Otto's is Bouquet, which according to *Cincinnati Magazine*, has "a rustic, soulful quality" because it's committed to using seasonal ingredients, and if something runs out, the chef moves on to something else to be obtained locally. "The flavors at Bouquet," the magazine wrote, "are about doing justice with what's available." Preparations are simple and straightforward. Places like these make Covington a destination for serious diners.

Mainstrasse, Covington, KY

TAKE A SPIN
THROUGH CRAFT BEER HEAVEN

A craft beer revolution keeps growing in Cincinnati, inspired by the city's German beer history. In fact, Boston Brewing's major brewery for Sam Adams is here with a recently added tap room. But the locals are truly offering fantastic choices, and more neighborhood breweries open up regularly. Sign up for a five-hour Brewery Tasting Tour with Cincy Brew Bus for an overview. Stops vary, but they routinely visit some of these locations: Rhinegeist Brewery (the "Ghost of the Rhine" has about a dozen lines, with Truth IPA and Cheetah lager being the most popular), MadTree Brewing Company (PsycHOPathy IPA), Taft's Ale House (in a renovated Over-the-Rhine church; check out Nellie's Key Lime Caribbean Ale, or Gavel Banger Double IPA), Braxton Brewing (Tropic Flare IPA), Esoteric Brewing in Walnut Hills (Lotus IPA), Streetside Brewery in the East End (Suh, Brah? IPA), Listermann Brewing Company (Triple Digit), Urban Artifact (Gadget Sour), and Fifty West Brewing (Doom Pedal White Ale).

Cincy Brew Bus
513-258-7909
cincybrewbus.com

MAKE LIKE MARIE ANTOINETTE
WITH CAKE FROM THE BONBONERIE

Since 1983, The BonBonerie specialty baker has been serving up wedding cakes and holiday treats for the most discriminating dessert hounds you know. Mary Pat Pace and Sharon Butler say their goal has been to have delicious food made with the best ingredients. It's hard to get beyond their Opera Cream Torte, a double chocolate chip cake filled and iced with vanilla opera cream and then coated with chocolate glaze, chocolate shavings, and white chocolate rosettes. There's also carrot cake to die for, handcrafted and specially decorated cookies and cupcakes, and a vast array of fine pastries—French macarons, English scones, double-fudge brownies, cheesecake cups, tarts, and even Whoopie Pie. This must be what they eat in heaven.

2030 Madison Rd., 513-321-3399
bonbonerie.com

TIP

Tea for two . . . or 22. BonBonerie's pleasant café can host up to 40 people, but the real treat is in the more intimate and private Tea Room (15–22 people), with eclectic chairs, a checkered floor, and more than 75 types of tea. Perfect for a shower or a special birthday. Book at least 24 hours in advance ($50 room rental, $25 per person).

LOOKING FOR A BUDDY (AND SOME PIZZA)?
CHECK IN AT LAROSA'S PIZZERIA

Buddy LaRosa used his Aunt Dena's recipe to make pizzas for a church festival in the early 1950s. They were a hit, so he opened his first pizzeria. The recently expanded pizzeria on Boudinot Avenue is where it all started. Today Buddy is the founder of one of Cincinnati's most legendary family-owned eateries with more than 60 pizzerias across Cincinnati, Northern Kentucky, Southeast Indiana, Dayton, and Columbus. Stop by for a pie topped with Dena's thick, sweet sauce. LaRosa's outsells several of the national chains in Greater Cincinnati. In addition to pizza, the menu features 40+ items: appetizers, calzones, pastas, salads, and hoagies, especially one called "The Baked Buddy," with capicola ham, pepperoni, salami, and provolone, with pizza sauce. It's the best!

2411 Boudinot Ave., Westwood
larosas.com

WHO MOVED THE CHEESE?
FIND OUT AT URBAN STEAD

Scott and Andrea Robbins make artisanal cheeses: Cheddar, Gouda, Camembert, Swiss, Quark (a German cream cheese and cheese curds, also called "squeakers"), and other artisanal cheeses. On several mornings every week they use 6,000 pounds of milk from an Ohio Valley farmer. They're keeping things local and sustaining a renewable cycle. Their leftover whey, a watery protein by-product from making cheese, goes to another farmer to feed his livestock. In their pleasant retail space in Walnut Hills, you can also order from a full bar with a selection of cheese and charcuterie plates. Families often come in with kids to watch cheese being made. They can see the Robbins's large round Goudas, cheddars, and more, aging in glass-walled, temperature-controlled rooms. They're for sale, of course, but their products are also exported to dozens of local restaurants and shops.

3036 Woodburn Ave., Evanston, 513-828-0830
urbansteadcheese.com

DRINK LIKE GERMANS
AT HOFBRÄUHAUS NEWPORT

Established in Munich, Germany, in 1589 by Wilhelm V, the Duke of Bavaria, the brewery Hofbräu München became renowned for its famed Weissbier ("wheat beer"). In 1810, the brewery launched the city's world-famous Oktoberfest celebration, replicated around the world. In 1997, they began to export beer to America. At the beginning of the 21st century, Newport, Kentucky, was chosen for America's first Hofbräuhaus thanks to Greater Cincinnati's heritage as a home for German immigrants from Munich and Bavaria. (Munich and Cincinnati are sister cities.) The Newport location features a brew house, a beer hall, and a beer garden modeled on the Munich original. With oompah polka bands, there's plenty of opportunities for hearty singing. And costumed servers wearing traditional Bavarian dirndl blouses and lederhosen ("leather breeches") delivering schnitzel, goulash, sauerbraten, and käsespätzle recreate an authentic, savory trip to Deutschland.

200 E 3rd St., Newport, 859-491-7200
hofbrauhausnewport.com

TIP

Since 1865, Mecklenburg Gardens has been a local spot for German immigrants to gather for food and drink. In its leafy, shaded beer garden, German heritage groups still gather to speak the language and sample lagers, dunkels, and hefeweizen—not to mention the "wursts"—bratwurst, mettwursts, and even a "goettawurst." (Check out No. 3)

302 E University Ave., 513-221-5353
mecklenburgs.com

THE EAGLE OTR
DELIVERS CINCINNATI'S BEST CHICKEN

Mail is no longer sent through the retired post office on Vine Street in Over-the-Rhine, but hungry diners line up there for stellar fried chicken from the Eagle Food and Beer Hall—sometimes waiting an hour or two for a table. Remnants of the past are reminders of the location's former existence: a bald eagle mural inspired by the historic post office logo as well as a wall of bronzed post office boxes. Not far from the Mason-Dixon Line (aka the Ohio River, about a mile south), Cincinnati's favorite destination for Southern fried chicken prepares cage-free, free-roaming, all-natural chicken that's brined, dredged, then dropped into custom-built fryers. The succulent result is served with spicy honey for a little extra kick. Don't miss the Southern side dishes made in-house: collards, spoonbread, sweet potatoes, grits, or succotash. Once won't be enough: You'll be back.

1342 Vine St., Over-the-Rhine, 513-802-5007
eaglerestaurant.com

TIP

Skip the line and avoid the wait by dropping in to Citybird, the Eagle's streamlined carry-out venture, first launched next door to the flagship food and beer hall. Success has led to three more locations where you can pick up an order of chicken tenders with craft sauces: Lemon Thyme Ranch, Green Chile Hot, Hot Honey Dijo, and the signature City Sauce.

1344 Vine St., Over-the-Rhine, 513-864-5720
11309 Montgomery Rd., Ste. D, Harper's Point, 513-387-0520
7893 Beechmont Ave, Anderson, 513-388-5330
2887 Dixie Hwy., Crestview Hills, KY, 859-578-1980
citybirdtenders.com

GET HIGH
ON A ROOFTOP BAR

We're talking elevation, not inebriation. There's something special about enjoying a glass of wine, a cocktail, or a craft beer from atop a downtown Cincinnati building. You might see people scurrying along the streets below, glimpse architectural details you miss from street level, or maybe see a barge creeping along the Ohio River. A few of these places were specifically designed, but more were carved out of mundane rooftops that now offer panoramic views of the city's picturesque downtown. Arrive early to get a seat or show up late when the air is breezy and cool. There's likely to be a crowd, but that's part of the fun, too.

21c Cocktail Terrace
609 Walnut St., Metropole Hotel, Downtown, 513-578-6600
21cmuseumhotels.com/cincinnati/fooddrink/cocktail-terrace

Top of the Park, The Phelps
506 E 4th St., Downtown
513-651-1234
topoftheparkcincinnati.com

AC Upper Deck
135 Joe Nuxhall Way, The Banks
513-744-9900
acupperdeck.com

Vista at Lytle Park
311 Pike St., Lytle Park Hotel
Downtown, 513-621-4500
thelytleparkhotel.com

The View at Shires Garden
309 Vine St., Downtown
513-407-7501
theviewatshiresgarden.com

Aster
8 E 4th St., Downtown, 513-381-4483
asteronfourth.com

NO NEED TO WAFFLE:
HEAD TO TASTE OF BELGIUM

In 2007, Jean-François Flechet came to Cincinnati with a 120-pound cast-iron waffle maker from his native Belgium. From a waffle cart at fairs to a stall at Findlay Market, he eventually expanded to four locations around town, as well as at Great American Ball Park. Made individually using thick dough and a coarse Belgian beet sugar that caramelizes inside the waffle iron, the result is sweet, dense, and heavenly. Have one with Banana and Nutella or ricotta cream and fruit, or pair it with a chicken breast, Ohio maple syrup, and hot sauce for a special treat. Taste of Belgium's first location, in Over-the-Rhine, has a pleasant bar, a bakery case—and a late-night brunch on Fridays and Saturdays (11 p.m.–1 a.m.). And don't miss another Belgian treat on Tuesdays: All-you-can-eat mussels and frites, while supplies last, beginning at 5 p.m.

Findlay Market, 1801 Race St.
Over-the-Rhine, 1135 Vine St.
The Banks, 16 W Freedom Way, Downtown
Rookwood, 3825 Edwards Rd.
Other locations in Kenwood, Mason, Liberty Twp., and Crestview Hills, KY
513-396-5800
authenticwaffle.com

TRY
WISPY-THIN PANCAKES
AT SUGAR N' SPICE

For more than 80 years, this homey diner in Bond Hill has served hearty breakfasts and lunches (open 7 a.m. to 3 p.m.)—everything from huge fluffy omelets to burgers and overstuffed sandwiches, such as the "Cuddlin' Puppy" (a kosher hot dot wrapped in bacon with American cheese and relish on Texas toast). In 2020, a second location was added in a classic diner in Over-the-Rhine, where those "original wispy-thin" pancakes are also available. Lighter than air, they don't seem like they'll fill you up, so you just have a few more. These are friendly, neighborly places where you'll find an always diverse crowd—college students, families, urban pioneers, grandparents, construction works, and lawyers.

4381 Reading Rd., Bond Hill, 513-242-3521
1203 Sycamore St., Over-the-Rhine, 513-762-0390
eatsugarnspice.com

DRINK SOME BREWING HISTORY
AT MOERLEIN LAGER HOUSE

Beer is king in Cincinnati, and the royalty began with Christian Moerlein, a German brewer who settled here in 1841 and began brewing hearty European beers in 1853. His brewery flourished for a half-century and was among the 10 largest American breweries by volume, but it closed in 1919 when Prohibition was imposed. The bright lager was resuscitated in 1981 and won a major brewing award, the Rhineheitsgebot, the German Beer Purity Law. Today at the Moerlein Lager House, adjacent to Great American Ball Park, you'll find an extensive tap list of numerous house-made drafts including the Original Lager, Se7en Hefeweizen, Barbaraossa (a Munich Dunkel), and Orange Cream Daydream (a cream ale). There are also guest drafts including Guinness Stout. The menu offers hearty sandwiches, oversized burgers, seafood, manly meat, soups, and salads.

115 Joe Nuxhall Way, The Banks, Downtown, 513-421-2337
moerleinlargerhouse.com

TAKE IN THE VIEW WITH YOUR FAVORITE DATE
AT PRIMAVISTA

You're going to get a fine Italian meal at Primavista, located in the burgeoning neighborhood of East Price Hill. But what really sets this place apart is the view from the restaurant's high promontory, as its name implies. The two-tiered dining room provides a panoramic view of Downtown Cincinnati, about a mile east. If you're there during a thunderstorm, it's like being in Mother Nature's greatest fireworks display. Primavista is generally considered one of the city's most romantic eateries.

Nearby is the Incline Public House, a more casual eatery sharing the sweeping vista from the hilltop where a Cincinnati incline landed in the late 19th century. Both places are good stops if you're seeing a show at the Warsaw Federal Incline Theatre across Matson Place.

Primavista
810 Matson Pl., East Price Hill, 513-251-6467
pvista.com

Incline Public House
2601 W 8th St., Price Hill, 513-251-3000
inclinepublichouse.com

COUNT TOOTHPICKS
AT POMPILIO'S RESTAURANT

Remember Dustin Hoffman's performance as autistic Raymond in the Academy Award–winning *Rain Man* (1988)? There's a scene when a dispenser of toothpicks spills on the floor of a restaurant—and he knows exactly how many have landed. The eatery where that happened is Pompilio's Restaurant in Newport, serving homey traditional Italian fare since 1933. (The 1902 building was a bar for three decades before that.) At the corner of Sixth Street and Washington Avenue, the owners call it an Italian restaurant with a Kentucky flavor, set in a historic neighborhood. It's where you want to go if you're yearning for such classics as lasagna, manicotti, rigatoni Bolognese, veal parmigiana, chicken cacciatore, and cannelloni. Mangia! (And there are still a few toothpicks.)

600 Washington Ave., Newport, KY, 859-581-3065
pompiliosrestaurant.com

HAVE WORLD-FAMOUS RIBS
AT MONTGOMERY INN BOATHOUSE

In 1951, this popular eatery started serving ribs and an iconic secret barbecue sauce (the secret recipe of restaurant founder Ted Gregory's wife, Matula) at a restaurant in the northern suburb of Montgomery. In 1989, they opened a second location, the Boathouse, adjacent to Cincinnati's International Friendship Park on the banks of the Ohio River. The sports-themed spots are always crowded. For nearly half a century, the restaurant was the nation's single biggest purchaser of loin back ribs; what's more, they ship 25,000 orders a year to addresses across America. Comedian Bob Hope so loved a meal from the cigar-chomping "Ribs King" that he had an order flown to him weekly in California for many years. But you can enjoy them right here in town.

Montgomery Inn
9440 Montgomery Rd., Montgomery, 513-791-3482

Boathouse
925 Riverside Dr., 513-721-7427

montgomeryinn.com

TIP
If you fall in love with Montgomery Inn's barbecue sauce, you can buy it by the bottle at the restaurant or in many local grocery stores.

GET DOWN
AT GHOST BABY

It's all downhill to find the unusual Ghost Baby bar, a unique, 170-year-old subterranean gathering place with moody lighting, craft cocktails, and live music. That's because it's four stories below Over-the-Rhine's Vine street in an underground lagering tunnel that was created by a 19th-century brewery to naturally cool and age the beer. In fact, you must look hard to find the entrance marked by two bright purple lamps, and then take an elevator down, down, and down. With the air of a speakeasy and a Prohibition nightclub, the space has drapes and chandeliers, high ceilings and arches. There are two rooms, the first with a small bar, the second, "The Den," has another bar, a stage, and seating for more than 100 people. It's certainly not down and out: It's an everchanging, unexpected, and unforgettable haunt.

1314 Republic St., Over-the-Rhine, 513-381-5333
ghost-baby.com

FOLLOW THE TRAIL
TO NEW RIFF DISTILLING

Bourbon is the much-prized drink of the Commonwealth of Kentucky, and its well-deserved tradition draws tourists and liquor fans from far and wide. As of 2014, Northern Kentucky had its own source when New Riff Distilling was founded. Aiming to be "a new riff on an old tradition," the sour mash whiskey distillery is crafting a range of products—bourbon and malted rye, as well as Kentucky Wild Gin. They are committed to the highest quality standard for their products, the Bottled in Bond Act of 1897. The family-owned business is already counted among the world's great small distilleries. Tours and events are available.

24 Distillery Way, Newport, KY, 859-261-7433
newriffdistilling.com

TIP

New Riff Distilling shares its parking lot with The Party Source, a supermarket-sized store for liquor, wine, craft beer, party goods, and more—a one-stop destination for more than 20,000 product selections. It's reputed to be one of the nation's largest liquor stores. Just browsing its aisles you'll discover an astonishing array of wines sorted by region and types, beers from craft breweries across America, and hard-to-find spirits. Keep an eye out for in-store tastings.

95 Riviera Dr., Bellevue, KY, 859-291-4007
thepartysource.com

SAMPLE AUTHENTIC MEXICAN FARE
AT MAZUNTE

This hidden gem's first location, in a strip mall between Oakley and Madisonville, opened in 2013. It blossomed into a catering business, a Kroger location, and, in early 2019, a second taqueria, Mazunte Centro. True culinary seekers zero in on Mazunte for fresh, flavorful fare from the southwestern Mexican state of Oaxaca that includes moles, enchiladas, empanadas, posole, (a hominy and pork stew) and tamales, as well as tacos (made with mahi-mahi). Mazunte's locations make their own salsa verde, pico de gallo, and more to serve as perfect prefaces to a meal. You'll find authentic Mexican food served with a serious commitment to quality—nothing stale, cold, fake, or bland. Sip a Mexican-bottled Coke, hot chocolate, sangria, or a margarita. And top it off with churros, deep-fried pastry coated with cinnamon sugar.

5207 Madison Rd., Madisonville, 513-785-0000
611 Main St., Downtown
mazuntetacos.com

Cincinnati Music Hall
Courtesy of Joanne Grueter

MUSIC
AND ENTERTAINMENT

SING YOUR HEART OUT
AND MAKE FRIENDS

Cincinnatians love to sing—dating back more than 150 years when German immigrants staged *singvereins*, choral singing events that brought friends together to vocalize. The granddaddy of them all, the Cincinnati May Festival, kicked off in the spring of 1873, making it the oldest choral festival in the Western Hemisphere. It's still going strong for two weeks every May, with 130 powerful voices. They also share the Music Hall stage whenever the Cincinnati Symphony needs a chorus. In 2012, the Young Professionals' Choral Collective assembled to sing Christmas carols and quickly grew to nearly 1,200 volunteers, 21 to 45, who sign up in smaller groups for programs requiring six weeks of rehearsal (enhanced by outings to neighborhood bars) and performances in neighborhood venues. Between these two poles are numerous outlets, from the highly professional Vocal Arts Ensemble (a 25-voice chamber choir) to the Cincinnati Boychoir (200 boys, ages 6 to 18, in seven ensembles) and MUSE, a diverse feminist choir (60 voices).

May Festival, Music Hall
1241 Elm St., Over-the-Rhine, 513-381-3300
mayfestival.com

Young Professionals'
Choral Collective
ypccsing.org

Vocal Arts Ensemble, Music Hall
1241 Elm St., 513-381-3300
vaecinci.org

MUSE, Cincinnati's Women's Choir, 513-221-1118
musechoir.org

ENJOY AUTHENTIC BLUEGRASS TUNES
AT THE COMET

Appalachian music is woven into the culture of Greater Cincinnati, and its greatest local proponents are The Comet Bluegrass All-Stars, the house band at the Northside neighborhood bar The Comet. But they frequently entertain audiences in much larger venues (including Cincinnati Music Hall with the renowned Cincinnati Pops Orchestra), and they've released five excellent, well-received recordings of bluegrass tunes, including one titled *A New Kind of Lonesome*. The six-musician band—everyone plays and sings—has a regular gig every Sunday night in Northside, when you can also enjoy The Comet's famous burritos with some musical hot licks.

4579 Hamilton Ave., Northside, 513-541-8900
cometbar.com, cometbluegrass.com

GROOVE WITH MUSIC IN THE GREAT OUTDOORS
AT RIVERBEND

The Riverbend Music Center is where Cincinnatians head for music in the summertime. The Cincinnati Symphony and Pops orchestras play concerts in the Michael Graves–designed pavilion, on the picturesque banks of the Ohio River, 10 miles east of Downtown. (If the river rises, it floods—but seldom in the summer.) Riverbend is where singer-songwriter Jimmy Buffett has entertained thousands of "Parrotheads" every year since 1988. Pop and country music stars swing through, including Dave Matthews Band, The Chicks, and James Taylor, for crowds up to 20,000 or so. There's a smaller venue next door (the PNC Bank Pavilion, seating 4,100, no lawn), where yesteryear's bands and music makers appear (for example, Beach Boys, Four Tops, Don Henley, Lyle Lovett, Barenaked Ladies, and more). Get your tunes on here.

6295 Kellogg Ave., 513-232-5882
riverbend.org

TIP

If you enjoy outdoor music venues, you have two great choices close to the Ohio River near Downtown. At The Banks, adjacent to the Bengals' Paycor Stadium, is the Andrew J. Brady Music Center (4,500 seats), while in Newport you'll find the MegaCorp Pavilion (5,000 seats) within the Ovation development. Both concert sites host performances by touring rock & roll bands, and both have flexible indoor and outdoor options.

Andrew J. Brady Music Center: 25 Race St., The Banks 513-232-5882, bradymusiccenter.com

MegaCorp Pavilion: 101 W 4th St., Newport, KY 859-900-2294, promowestlive.com/cincinnati/ megacorp-pavilion

OOH AND AHH
AT SPECTACULAR
FIREWORKS
ON THE BANKS OF THE OHIO

Riverfest is Cincinnati's way of saying goodbye to summer. Estimates have it that a half-million people flock to the north and south banks of the Ohio on Labor Day weekend's Sunday evening for the WEBN Fireworks, after a daylong event with music and hanging out on boats and the shore. The rock-and-roll radio station creates a timely soundtrack and partners with Rozzi Famous Fireworks (a world leader for inventive pyrotechnics since 1895 that's brightened the skies of the White House) for a 30-minute extravaganza featuring hundreds of aerial shots launched from river barges and employing Ohio River bridges for special displays. (The "Niagara Falls" effect is a longtime favorite.) A TV station typically broadcasts the show, but you really should be there with the crowd and the radio cranked up. The deafening finale will make your heart beat faster. Free admission.

Riverfest, The Banks of the Ohio River, 513-352-4000

SHAKE OFF THE WINTER BLUES
AT BOCKFEST

For three decades, local beer fans have celebrated Bockfest in early March, a grassroots community event managed by the Brewery District Community Urban Redevelopment Corporation. Typically the first weekend of March, Bockfest kicks off with a wacky, irreverent Friday evening parade starting at Arnold's Bar & Grill and winding its merry way up Main Street through Over-the-Rhine to the Bockfest Hall (found in various locations annually). All weekend celebrants can indulge in an array of specially crafted bock beers, typically amber in color with robust malt flavors. These dark brews, stronger than typical lagers, were first brewed by Bavarian monks in 17th-century Germany to mark the passage of winter to spring. A "bock" is a billy goat, the mascot for the Cincinnati festivities.

bockfest.com

Managed by Brewery District CURC
1939 Race St., Ste. C101, 513-604-9812
brewerydistrict.org

GO DEUTSCH AND DO THE CHICKEN DANCE
AT OKTOBERFEST

Cincinnati's German roots are particularly on display during Oktoberfest-Zinzinnati, the largest Oktoberfest in the United States. More than one in four area residents have German heritage (on the city's West Side, neighborhoods are roughly 50 percent German). So everyone goes "Deutsch" for the annual mid-September event, which kicks off with the "Running of the Wieners," 100 dachshunds wearing hot-dog bun costumes and racing for top honors. That hilarious event is followed by three days of food, music, and—of course—lots of beer! Streets are closed to traffic and lined with food and beer booths, vendors, and bands playing in five different beer gardens. More than 500,000 people throng through four blocks of Downtown Cincinnati. No charge for admission.

Cincinnati USA Regional Chamber, 513-579-3100
oktoberfestzinzinnati.com

TIP

Don your lederhosen and shake your booty in the World's Largest Chicken Dance, officially recorded by the Guinness Book of Records with 48,000 participants! Every year, celebrities are chosen to lead the crowd on Downtown Cincinnati's Fountain Square—from the Crown Prince of Bavaria and Weird Al Yankovic, as well as TV "star" Homer Simpson and *Star Trek*'s Mr. Sulu, George Takei.

GET WEIRD DURING THE CINCINNATI FRINGE FESTIVAL
AT KNOW THEATRE

For two weeks every summer, kicking off right after Memorial Day, the Cincinnati Fringe Festival presents 40-plus experimental theater and dance productions, a total of nearly 200 performances annually in a dozen theaters, bars, churches, coffee shops, and storefronts throughout the Over-the-Rhine neighborhood. Local creators, national touring artists, and even international performers put on shows and entertainment. Productions tend to be bare bones, but they're always entertaining—some serious, some hilarious, some just plain weird. Take a chance and you're sure to see something memorable.

1120 Jackson St., Over-the-Rhine, 513-300-5669
cincyfringe.com

TIP

After each evening's Fringe performances, there are post-show special events in the Underground Bar, at Know Theatre, the festival's organizer—everything from Fringe Olympics, Fringe-a-Oke, and even a Fringe Prom. It's a chance to meet and mingle with performers.

SWING AND SWAY ON A SHARK BRIDGE
AT THE NEWPORT AQUARIUM

A family-friendly underwater experience awaits visitors to Newport on the Levee. On the western edge of the shopping complex's large plaza, a visit will find lots of exotic aquatic creatures—fish, of course, but also white alligators and even playful penguins. An underwater glass tunnel gives visitors the experience of walking the ocean floor surrounded by aquatic life, even sharks. Particularly memorable is the thrilling first-in-the-world Shark Bridge, a rope span (with high sides) that guests can cross inches above a tank full of sharks. In a shallow tide pool, kids can touch sea urchins, live starfish, and rays. "The Shipwreck: Realm of the Eels" is populated by slithering creatures who have found an accidental reef home in an ancient sunken ship. And for the holidays, Scuba Santa is not to be missed, swimming in a tank full of sharks with his elf friends.

1 Aquarium Way, Newport, KY, 800-406-3474
newportaquarium.com

BEAT THE ODDS
AT HARD ROCK CASINO

Cincinnati's $400 million gambling venue began life in 2013 as Horseshoe Casino. During 2016 it changed to Jack Cincinnati Casino, and in 2019 it became Hard Rock Casino, but the name changes are more about ownership than operations. It's easy to find on Downtown's northeast corner; look for the 80-foot sign. Open most days from 9 a.m. to 1 a.m.; on Fridays and Saturdays, hang out until 3 a.m. (Parking is free.) With 2,000 slot machines and 85 gambling tables, you have plenty of ways to "invest." Serious gamblers like the World Series of Poker room, with 31 tables. The sure bets at the casino are an array of great restaurants; because of the casino's design, many are accessible without entering the gaming floor. No kids, by the way: You have to be 21 to enter.

1000 Broadway St., 513-250-3150
hardrockcasinocincinnati.com

WITNESS A MEDIEVAL HOLIDAY PAGEANT
AT CHRIST CHURCH CATHEDRAL

The Boar's Head and Yule Log Festival is an ancient holiday celebration from the Middle Ages. Its 600th anniversary was in 1940, the year Christ Church first marked it in Cincinnati. Rooted in pagan traditions, filtered through Christianity in 14th-century England and colonial America, the ceremony happens shortly after Christmas and New Year's Day, during the Epiphany season. It features period costumes and music from the Middle Ages as performers—"Beefeaters," lords, ladies, knights, minstrels, cooks, hunters, and pages—process into the downtown church's sanctuary with singing of carols and solemn pageantry. Before it's over, there are angels, the Magi, shepherds, and more. The cast of 150 is supported by a crew of 70 behind the scenes. It's the Episcopal congregation's annual gift to the city. Free tickets are distributed in early December.

Christ Church Cathedral
318 E 4th St., ticket hotline: 513-621-2627
boarsheadfestival.com

GET THE MEMO
FOR GREAT EVENTS

Built in 1908 by the Grand Army of the Republic to commemorate veterans of the Civil and Spanish-American wars (look for statues of historic soldiers above the front doors), Memorial Hall languished for nearly 50 years without air conditioning or adequate restroom facilities. Thanks to an $11 million renovation, the stately Beaux Arts–style building was reborn in 2016 as another attractive entertainment venue, sitting next to Cincinnati Music Hall along Over-the-Rhine's bustling Elm Street arts corridor. There's a 556-seat, second-floor proscenium theater with marble staircases, decorative murals, rails, and Tiffany-style light fixtures, as well as two accommodating ballrooms on the first floor and a basement studio for informal performances and meetings. These changes make "The Memo" a popular destination for concerts, improv comedy, movies, weddings, corporate events, and more. Check the online schedule for details of events.

Memorial Hall
1225 Elm St., Over-the-Rhine, 513-977-8837
memorialhallotr.com

ENJOY OPERA OR A SYMPHONY CONCERT
AT CINCINNATI MUSIC HALL

A National Historic Landmark, Cincinnati Music Hall is one of North America's most venerated concert venues. The gorgeous Victorian Gothic structure was built in 1878 (on a site that was once a public cemetery) for German singing festivals. Its north and south halls hosted agricultural and industrial exhibitions. It hosted the 1888 Republican National Convention, nominating Benjamin Harrison, America's 23rd president. The "People's Palace" received a spectacular $143 million facelift in 2016 and 2017, restoring historic interiors and refurbishing and relighting exterior facades. It's the destination for concerts by the Cincinnati Symphony Orchestra (which began in 1895) and Pops, performances like *The Nutcracker* by Cincinnati Ballet, and productions by Cincinnati Opera, which staged summer shows in an amphitheater at the Cincinnati Zoo starting in 1920, then moved indoors at the Music Hall in 1970.

1241 Elm St., Over-the-Rhine, 513-621-2787
cincinnatiarts.org/music-hall

TIP

To learn more about this beautiful
building, turn to volunteer tour guides
from the Friends of Music Hall. They will
take you backstage, through the majestic
performance hall, and give you a glimpse of
the Mighty Wurlitzer theater organ (once in
a long-gone Downtown movie theater, now
installed in Music Hall's Ballroom).

513-744-3293

If paranormal activity intrigues you,
look for occasional two-hour ghost tours via
cincinnatiarts.org/events/detail/ghost-tours

WATCH MUSICAL THEATER TALENT TRAIN FOR BROADWAY
AT CCM

The University of Cincinnati's College-Conservatory of Music has a musical theater training program that's considered one of the top three in the United States. Every year they select 20 promising high school grads (after auditioning 800 talented prospects) and give them the kind of professional training it takes to break in and become a Broadway star. They perform on three professional-level stages in shows that are familiar (*Carousel, Into the Woods, Les Misérables*) and lesser known (*American Idiot, Lysistrata Jones, Big River*). Most grads are in Broadway shows a year or two after graduating and become stars before long: 2004 grad Betsy Wolfe played Princess Elsa in the 2018 Broadway production of Disney's *Frozen*! Other famous CCM alums include Ashley Brown, Faith Prince, and composer Stephen Flaherty. Production runs are brief (generally one weekend), so keep an eye on the schedule.

CCM Village, University of Cincinnati, Clifton, 513-556-4813
ccm.uc.edu

FIND OUT
WHAT'S NEW IN DANCE
FROM CINCINNATI BALLET

Not many cities today have full-time professional ballet companies. If they do, their repertoire is likely to be classical, tutus, and toe shoes. Cincinnati Ballet likes to push the boundaries. They do that particularly with the Kaplan New Works Series at the Aronoff Center that annually celebrates innovation in dance, bringing internationally respected choreographers to town. Works vary from year to year, but they are always cutting edge. One season celebrated the company's accomplished women dancers performing works by female choreographers. This company of approximately two dozen professional women and men from around the world is all about the power and passion of dance, and New Works is the greatest distillation of that commitment.

Jarson-Kaplan Theater, Aronoff Center for the Arts
650 Walnut St., 513-621-5219
cballet.org

SEE AN INDIE MOVIE
AT THE ESQUIRE OR THE MARIEMONT

Every city needs a movie house showing art films, indie productions, and subtitled foreign films, and Cincinnati has a pair. The "original" location is the Esquire, a longtime theater in a quaint business, restaurant, and bar strip near the University of Cincinnati, but you'll find many similar films at the Mariemont Theatre on Cincinnati's East Side. Keep an eye out for offbeat selections, including midnight showings of *The Rocky Horror Picture Show* at the Esquire.

Esquire
320 Ludlow Ave., Clifton
esquiretheatre.com

Mariemont Theatre
6906 Wooster Pike, Mariemont
mariemonttheatre.com

TIP

Popular opinion has it that the Esquire and the Mariemont serve the best, freshest popcorn of any movie theater in Cincinnati.

Sawyer Point Pickleball Courts
Courtesy of Cincinnati Pickleball Club

SPORTS
AND RECREATION

JOIN PADDLEFEST
ON THE OHIO RIVER

On a pleasant Sunday morning in August, shove off from a point nine miles east of Downtown Cincinnati with more than 1,400 canoe and kayak enthusiasts for the annual Paddlefest. You'll pass under six bridges, take in the skylines of Cincinnati and Northern Kentucky, and race or drift downstream to Cincinnati's Public Landing. Some compete, some go with the flow: either way, it's a fine summer outing that encompasses an entire weekend, including events for kids managed by Adventure Crew, a nonprofit organization that connects city teens with nature through recreation, education, and conservation activities.

Ohio River Paddlefest
1662 Blue Rock St.
ohioriverpaddlefest.org, adventurecrew.org

HANG OUT WITH WORLD-CLASS TENNIS PLAYERS
AT THE WESTERN & SOUTHERN OPEN

The annual Western & Southern Open is one of America's premier tennis tournaments, a chance for fans to get up close and personal with contemporary greats of the court. Its roots go back to 1899; competitions in the early decades of the 20th century featured some of the era's most well-known tennis players. The tournament became an ATP men's event in 1979, the same year it moved to Mason, Ohio, 25 miles north of Downtown Cincinnati. Women competitors gained equal status with the men starting with the 2004 tournament. The Lindner Family Tennis Center is one of the best in America, with four permanent stadiums and 17 courts providing seating for nearly 10,000 tennis enthusiasts. Tournament attendance routinely tops 200,000. It's two weeks of celebrities and media, parties and receptions, plus a gourmet food court.

Western & Southern Open, Lindner Family Tennis Center
5460 Courseview Dr., Mason, 513-651-0303
wsopen.com

LACE UP
YOUR RUNNING SHOES
FOR THE FLYING PIG MARATHON

Back in the 1800s when Cincinnati was a big deal in meat processing, pigs were often run through the Downtown streets, earning the city a nickname: Porkopolis. Today, it is people who are running the streets and hills of Cincinnati in the annual Flying Pig Marathon—nearly 40,000 participants, in fact—on the first Sunday of May. If you're not ready for 26.2 miles, there's a half-marathon, a 10K, a 5K, several relays, and a kids' division. There's even a "Flying Fur" event for dogs and humans. Even if you don't run, you can be an active spectator—cheering on participants or joining the thousands who make the event run like, well, a marathoner.

Marathon Office
644 Linn St., Ste. 626, 513-721-7447
flyingpigmarathon.com

TIP

The Flying Pig is a certified course and a Boston Marathon qualifier. Typically, more than 200 runners qualify for Boston.

MAKE SOME HITS
AT LOCAL PICKLEBALL COURTS

No matter where you live in Cincinnati, you're probably not too far from a court to play pickleball, that hybrid between ping-pong and tennis. It's the fastest-growing sport in the United States. Sawyer Point's long under-utilized tennis courts on the banks of the Ohio River east of downtown have been transformed into 20 pickleball courts, free of charge for those eager to ping plastic balls back and forth. (There's even a ball machine for those in need of perfecting their "dinking.") The city invested $509,000 in 2022 to turn this into a showplace. (Several tennis courts were preserved, too.) That's not the only place to pick up a game: In fact, the second-largest indoor pickleball facility in the United States has been established in West Chester: The Pickle Lodge—with 17 indoor courts and five outdoor courts, plus a bar, a restaurant, and a group event space. Both facilities feature multi-layered, flexible asphalt playing surfaces with state-of-the-art sound and lighting.

Pickleball at Sawyer Point
815 E Pete Rose Way, 513-352-6180
pbatsp.com

The Pickle Lodge
7373 Kingsgate Way, West Chester, 513-777-5530
thepicklelodge.com

STARGAZE
AT THE CINCINNATI OBSERVATORY

Budding astronomers and inveterate space watchers love to visit to the oldest professional observatory in the United States. Cincinnati's original observatory was first located in Mount Adams, so named when former President John Quincy Adams came to lay the cornerstone in 1843. In 1873, to escape Downtown's smoke and dirt, the observatory moved to Mount Lookout. One building houses the 1845 wood-and-brass *Merz und Mahler* 11-inch refractor telescope, likely the oldest continually used telescope in the world; an adjacent building houses a 16-inch refractor from 1904. Both are used for public education programs and graduate research. You can tour weekdays between noon and 4 p.m., or monthly on the second and fourth Sunday afternoons, 1-4 p.m. Especially informative are visits on most Thursday and Friday nights and some Saturday nights with an astronomer and a chance to peer into outer space.

3489 Observatory Pl., Mount Lookout, 513-321-5186
cincinnatiobservatory.org

TIP
The Cincinnati Observatory's outreach astronomer, Dean Regas, co-hosts the PBS series *Star Gazers* as well as a blog, *Looking Up*, with new episodes distributed twice monthly by WVXU-FM 91.7.

WHEEL AROUND CINCINNATI
AND NORTHERN KENTUCKY

Multiple alternative modes of transportation are everywhere. Bikes are big all around Cincinnati, with excellent trails in Loveland, Glendale, and other suburban communities. The City of Cincinnati has created bike lanes on numerous thoroughfares enabling two-wheeled transportation around the city's core. No bike of your own? Check out Cincinnati Red Bike. The bike-sharing program offers dozens of docking stations around Downtown, Over-the-Rhine, and UC, as well as Covington, Newport, and Bellevue, Kentucky. A day pass is just $8, enabling you to ride for 60-minute increments. Scooters by Bird (www.bird.co) and Lime (www.li.me) are rentable two-wheelers ($1 to unlock, 15¢ per minute to ride), found throughout the urban core and beyond. They're a quick alternative to run errands or sightsee without hassles or emissions. No searching for parking, either. Riders should stay off sidewalks and wear a helmet for safety. Easy-to-use apps are available for each.

Cincinnati Red Bike, 513-621-2453
cincyredbike.org

DIG INTO CINCINNATI'S BASEBALL HISTORY
AT THE REDS HALL OF FAME

The Cincinnati Reds were the first professional baseball team. (They were called the Red Stockings back in 1869.) That's a history to celebrate, and the best place to do it is at the Reds Hall of Fame & Museum. Established in 1958, it's the oldest team hall of fame in baseball. More than 85 inductees are now honored in the 16,000-square-foot space adjacent to Great American Ball Park. You'll find lots of interactive displays for kids to enjoy, plus memorabilia, photos, and videos of the legendary Big Red Machine that won back-to-back World Series in 1975 and 1976. In 2016, Pete Rose, one of the greatest Reds players ever—who grew up on Cincinnati's West Side—was inducted. A 50-foot "wall of balls" uses 4,256 baseballs to represent the number of hits during his career.

100 Joe Nuxhall Way, 513-765-7923
cincinnati.reds.mlb/cin/hof

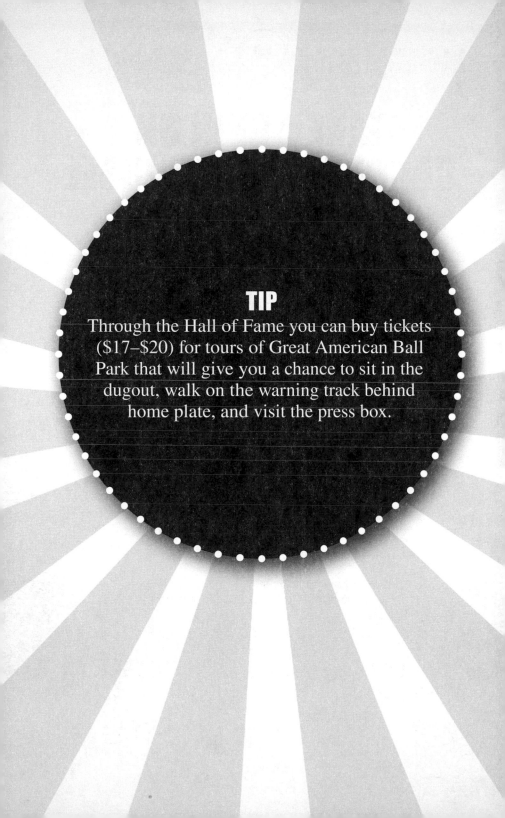

TIP

Through the Hall of Fame you can buy tickets ($17–$20) for tours of Great American Ball Park that will give you a chance to sit in the dugout, walk on the warning track behind home plate, and visit the press box.

TAKE A SPIN ON CAROL ANN'S CAROUSEL
AT SMALE RIVERFRONT PARK

Carol Ann Haile and her husband, Ralph, left a legacy that's advanced life in Greater Cincinnati for years. The most visible evidence is a carousel named in her honor that began enchanting families in 2015 at Smale Riverfront Park, surrounded by playgrounds, gardens, cafés, and more. It features 44 characters representing the region's life, history, and culture. The hand-carved, painted figures were inspired by ideas proposed by area residents—an Oktoberfest horse, a Carew Tower gorilla, a Porkopolis pig, a UC Bearcat, an Ohio cardinal, a Bengal tiger for football, and a white tiger representing the Cincinnati Zoo. It's all enclosed in a beautiful glass pavilion, so it operates year-round. Look for fanciful panels on the carousel, with scenes from Cincinnati parks featuring some of the carousel figures. A two-and-a-half minute ride is $2.

100 W Mehring Way, 513-357-2621
mysmaleriverfrontpark.org/carousel.htm

HEAD TO THE MIDDLE AGES
AT THE LOVELAND CASTLE

The lifelong project of Harry D. Andrews is formally dubbed "Château Laroche," but most everyone calls this singlehanded structure "The Loveland Castle." Andrews was a World War I veteran and a lover of the Middle Ages. He began to assemble his castle on the banks of the Little Miami River in the 1920s, often using stones dredged from the riverbed. A Boy Scout leader, he took 50 years to complete this unusual building with the help of "The Knights of the Golden Trail," the troop he led. He willed the castle to them when he died in 1981, and it's been lovingly preserved with historic artifacts from Europe and beautifully maintained gardens. You can take a self-guided tour that includes a video about the construction process. A great visit for the kids.

12025 Shore Dr., Loveland, 513-683-4686
lovelandcast.com

SPEED AROUND TWISTS AND TURNS
AT KINGS ISLAND

Kings Island amusement park is 24 miles northeast of Downtown Cincinnati. Sprawling across 364 acres, the park has invested more than $275 million since 1972 to create 80 rides, shows, and attractions. The park attracts more than three million visitors annually, the second-highest attendance of any park in the United States. It's a mecca for roller coaster enthusiasts. The Beast, the legendary wooden coaster built in 1979, is one of the tallest and fastest in the world. In four minutes, you'll cover more than a mile of terrain, at speeds of up to 64 mph. The new Mystic Timbers has received rave reviews with 16 airtime moments. Vortex flings riders through a double corkscrew and a boomerang turn. The Banshee is the world's longest upside-down steel coaster, and The Diamondback features steep drops at 80 mph and a big splashdown. Open from early spring through Labor Day, as well as weekends in September through Halloween.

6300 Kings Island Dr., Mason, 513-754-5700
visitkingsisland.com

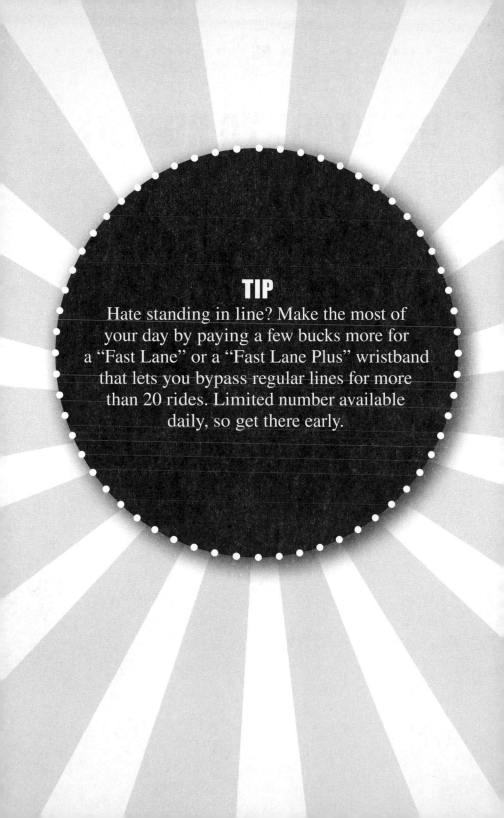

TIP

Hate standing in line? Make the most of your day by paying a few bucks more for a "Fast Lane" or a "Fast Lane Plus" wristband that lets you bypass regular lines for more than 20 rides. Limited number available daily, so get there early.

GET READY TO RUMBLE
IN "THE JUNGLE"

That's where dangerous animals prowl, and that's the nickname for Paycor Stadium, home of the NFL's Cincinnati Bengals, frequent contenders for the NFL playoffs who went to Super Bowl LVI in 2022. This contemporary stadium holds more than 65,000 fans, and lots of them have a good time on fall afternoons and evenings with pregame tailgating in the parking areas that surround the stadium on the Banks or at nearby bars and restaurants. The Bengals' big rivals are three teams from the American Football Conference's Central Division—the Cleveland Browns, the Baltimore Ravens, and the Pittsburgh Steelers. Wear your tiger stripes, die your hair orange, and get ready for some football.

Paycor Stadium
1 Paycor Stadium, 513-456-4800
bengals.com/stadium

TAKE A DIP IN A GIANT SWIMMING POOL
AT CONEY ISLAND

Since 1925, Cincinnatians have been swimming at Coney Island's Sunlite Pool, the nation's largest recirculating pool. Annual attendance is around 450,000. During the park's heyday before its owners opened Kings Island, attendance sometimes topped one million swimmers. It's 401 feet long, 200 feet wide (that's about two acres of water), and it takes three days to fill it with three million gallons of water—that's enough to fill 100,000 bathtubs! If you don't want to spend the whole day floating around, you can also enjoy attractions at Coney Island, a low-key but family-friendly amusement park with rides and waterslides. The pool is open June through Labor Day in September. Don't forget the sunscreen, since there's not a lot of shade.

6201 Kellogg Ave., 513-232-8230
coneyislandpark.com/sunlite-pool

GET FESTIVE (AND MAYBE DO SOME SHOPPING)
AT WASHINGTON PARK

Cincinnati's favorite greenspace is Over-the-Rhine's Washington Park, which began in 1855. It was significantly remodeled and improved in 2012. It now offers entertainment and festivals on the Great Lawn atop a 450-car underground parking garage opposite historic Music Hall. One of the best events is The City Flea, an original curated, monthly urban flea market from April through October with a special holiday edition in December. Cincinnati is teeming with artistic creativity, energy, and entrepreneurial spirit. Started in 2011, The City Flea is replete with locally produced merchandise from jewelry and vintage clothing to furniture and fiber art. Strolling through the 150 or so booths lined up across the spacious lawn, thousands of shoppers—with kids and dogs in tow—check out local artists and creators selling their clever crafts and inventive products. It's more than a monthly market: it's a small business incubator and city advocate. When festivals aren't happening, there's still the sheltered Porch with drink service and a wooden deck, adjacent to a bandstand and a kid-friendly water "sprayground."

Washington Park
1230 Elm St., Over-the-Rhine
513-621-4400
washingtonpark.org

The City Flea
thecityflea.com

EXPLORE ANCIENT INDIAN MOUNDS
VIA MORGAN'S CANOE LIVERY

If canoeing, kayaking, and rafting are your thing, you want to head to Morgan's Canoe Livery, the only outfitter in the Fort Ancient Gorge of the Little Miami River. An added benefit of this secluded section of river, beyond its natural beauty and isolation (you're about six miles away from much civilization), is its proximity to trails and grounds once frequented by the prehistoric Hopewell peoples, also known as "Mound Builders." You can enjoy some water activities from the livery and also visit Fort Ancient State Memorial Park, where you can observe ancient burial mounds. You can also hike or bike along the Little Miami Scenic Trail, the third-longest paved trail in the United States.

Morgan's Canoe Livery
5701 St. Rt. 350, Oregonia, 513-932-7658
morganscanoe.com

Fort Ancient State Memorial Park
6123 St. Rt. 350, Oregonia, 513-932-4843
fortancient.org

KICK AROUND AT A SOCCER MATCH
AT FC CINCINNATI'S TQL STADIUM

There are people who call soccer the sport of the future, but it's clear that the future has landed in Cincinnati with the ascendance of Futbol Club (FC) Cincinnati to a Major League Soccer (MLS) franchise. In fact, the club's new 26,500-seat TQL Stadium resembles a futuristic spaceship looming over Central Parkway just north of downtown. The team laid a solid foundation with several years of strong competition, making their elevation to the top tier a foregone conclusion. Tickets are reasonably priced for families, and FC Cincinnati is populated with top-notch international players from the USA, Argentina, Brazil, Cameroon, England, Jamaica, Japan, and Senegal. Fire up your vuvuzela, stop by a pub partner, and march to a match!

FC Cincinnati, TQL Stadium
1501 Central Pkwy., 513-977-5425
tqlstadium.com, fccincinnati.com

MAKE LIKE MARK TWAIN AND PLY THE OHIO
ON A RIVERBOAT

Once upon a time, paddle-wheeled riverboats traveled up and down the Ohio River, bringing new citizens to America's frontier—when Cincinnati was known as the "Queen City of the West." Those days are gone, but you can still enjoy riverboat cruises to see scenic views of the cities along the river. BB Riverboats features the *Belle of Cincinnati* and the *River Queen*, both outfitted for customer comfort (multi-level enclosed decks are air-conditioned) with lavish and romantic Victorian charm. Queen City Riverboats has tours as well as concert cruises to Riverbend Music Center and shuttles to Reds and Bengals games. Check out numerous cruise options—some include dining (most boats have on-board bars), and all afford excellent sightseeing augmented by knowledgeable commentary from the crew. Special trips happen during holidays, and the boats are popular options for birthday parties, weddings, private events, and charter cruises.

BB Riverboats
101 Riverboat Row, Newport, KY, 800-261-8586
bbriverboats.com

Queen City Riverboats
100 O'Fallon Ave., Dayton, KY, 859-292-8687

VISIT LEGENDARY THOROUGHBREDS
AT KENTUCKY HORSE PARK

Kentucky Horse Park is an easy day trip, 75 miles from Downtown Cincinnati down I-75 at exit 120, just north of Lexington, Kentucky. The park, established in 1978, features the world's best equine competition facilities that you can explore firsthand with tours on foot or horse-drawn. Equine presentations are available throughout most days, and you can visit the 60,000-square-foot International Museum of the Horse, plus the American Saddlebred Museum, the Al-Marah Arabian Horse Galleries, and the Wheeler Museum, focused on the "hunter/ jumper" industry. On the grounds are statues and remembrances of some of history's greatest racehorses, including a memorial to Man o' War (1917–1947), whose remains are buried there. There is a one-ticket admission, but other horse shows and special events take place frequently that might be separately ticketed. Horseplay is definitely encouraged here!

4089 Iron Works Pkwy., Lexington, KY, 859-233-4303
kyhorsepark.com, imh.org

CHEER FOR THE MUSKETEERS OR THE BEARCATS
AT THE CROSSTOWN SHOOTOUT

Cincinnati is a great town for college basketball. Both of the city's historic institutions of higher education, the University of Cincinnati and Xavier University have storied records in the sport. The campuses are just three miles from one another, and the UC Bearcats and the XU Musketeers have fiercely loyal fans for programs that are perennial frontrunners in NCAA competition. There have been contests between the schools since 1927, and they've played one another in the annual "Crosstown Shootout," one of the longest such rivalries in the United States since 1945. The contest alternates between the schools' top-notch arenas, XU's Cintas Center and UC's Fifth Third Arena. No matter whom you root for, you're bound to have a good time.

Tickets: gobearcats.com, goxavier.com

CAM Art Climb
Courtesy of Cincinnati Art Museum

CULTURE
AND HISTORY

PERUSE HISTORIC ADS
AT THE AMERICAN SIGN MUSEUM

Iconic business signs are an American tradition—think fast food's Golden Arches, roadside gas stations, Mail Pouch Tobacco on barns, neon on nightclubs, and more. The American Sign Museum has them all, celebrating two centuries of this varied art form, woven into our nation's personality. Hundreds of historic signs and outdoor advertising artifacts are on display in the nearly 40,000-square-foot facility in Camp Washington (on Cincinnati's near West Side), a onetime parachute factory. The museum traces the history of sign making and portrays varied environments, from big cities to small towns, from motels to barns, where signs have become integral components of our culture.

1330 Monmouth St., 513-541-6366
americansignmuseum.org

FEEL THE REALITY OF SLAVERY
AT THE FREEDOM CENTER

At the National Underground Railroad Freedom Center, you can stand inside a slave pen built in the early 1800s to temporarily hold enslaved people in chains before they were moved farther south for sale. It's deeply moving, a reminder of our nation's troubled past. The Underground Railroad wasn't really underground or a railroad. It was a network of circumspect routes followed by people seeking freedom. For many of them, crossing the Ohio River was their goal, and the Freedom Center (opened in 2004), situated on the river's bank south of Downtown Cincinnati, celebrates freedom's heroes from the 19th century to the present. More than 100,000 visitors come annually for exhibits and dialogue about freedom and human rights.

50 E Freedom Way, 513-333-7500 (877-648-4838)
freedomcenter.org

GET DRAMATIC
AT THE CINCINNATI PLAYHOUSE IN THE PARK

You don't have to travel to New York City to enjoy top-notch theatrical productions, thanks to Cincinnati's Tony Award–winning regional theater. Directors, designers, and actors from Broadway frequently work at the Playhouse, which was founded in 1960. It is indeed "in the Park," above Mt. Adams's Eden Park. Its Shelterhouse Stage was once a park building, and it's still visible inside the spacious lobby. Seating 225 patrons, this intimate space is where you'll find shows typical of Off-Broadway. A new main stage, Moe and Jack's Place—The Rouse Theatre—seats 540. It's where mainstream productions are staged, as well as world premieres and an annual production of *A Christmas Carol*, one of Cincinnati's favorite holiday attractions. The Playhouse also assembles excellent productions for young audiences, presented at schools and community centers throughout the year.

962 Mt. Adams Cir., 513-421-3888
cincyplay.com

WET YOUR WHISTLE
AT FOUNTAIN SQUARE

For nearly a century and a half, "The Genius of Water" has presided over Downtown Cincinnati's Fountain Square, gently showering a crowd of people whose lives depended on water. The nine-foot, two-ton female statue has been moved more than once, but she's now in a very central location and beautifully lit. Four figures around her base feature playful children with a dolphin, ducks, a snake, and a turtle, each a water fountain for drinking. The Tyler Davidson Fountain was commissioned in 1871 by businessman Henry Probasco to memorialize his brother-in-law and business partner. It was designed by German sculptor August von Kreling, cast in bronze in Munich, and then installed here. She dries out in the winter when an ice-skating rink is installed nearby, but she's back to life in time for baseball's opening day. All summer long there are concerts on the Fifth and Vine permanent stage.

Fountain Square, 5th and Vine Streets, Downtown

EXPLORE CINCINNATI'S HISTORIC CREATIVITY
AT THE CINCINNATI ART MUSEUM

Cincinnati was an important center for visual art in the 19th century. In 1880, it was the first city west of the Allegheny Mountains to establish a full-fledged art museum. Today, the Cincinnati Art Museum has more than 60,000 objects and is a respected institution with impressive holdings. In particular, the Cincinnati Wing, a permanent display of the city's art history dating back to 1788 and filling 15 galleries, features paintings by Frank Duveneck and Robert S. Duncanson, art pottery and tiles from Rookwood, and Mitchell & Rammelsburg wood-carved furniture. Best of all: General admission to the museum, located in Eden Park not far from Downtown, is always free, thanks to an endowment by local philanthropists. (Special exhibitions sometimes have modest entry fees.)

953 Eden Park Dr., 513-721-2787
cincinnatiartmuseum.org

TIP

The Art Climb from the corner of Gilbert Avenue and Eden Park Drive to the museum's front entrance atop the hill challenges museumgoers with 164 steps. These zig-zagging flights are interspersed with four art plazas for sculpture or musicians. Light beam structures guide users upward to the museum. The climb is great exercise, and the reward of great art when you ascend to the top is worth the effort.

HAVE A PICNIC
AMONG CINCINNATIANS FROM THE PAST AT SPRING GROVE CEMETERY

Spring Grove Cemetery got its start in 1845 when members of the Cincinnati Horticultural Society created a 733-acre cemetery and arboretum. It's the second-largest cemetery in the United States, a National Historic Landmark, and the final resting place for Revolutionary War veterans and Civil War generals, abolitionists, and business leaders, including William Procter and James Gamble, founders of the Procter & Gamble Company, and Barney Kroger, founder of America's largest chain of supermarkets, as well as politicians and Supreme Court justices. Its beautiful natural setting offers an expansive collection of more than 1,000 native and exotic plants and trees. It's as much a beautiful destination for the living as a final resting place—a site for picnics, weddings, and walking tours.

4521 Spring Grove Ave., 513-681-PLAN
springgrove.org

TIP
Treat yourself to a self-guided tour of Spring Grove. Maps can be picked up in the lobby at the main gate on Spring Grove Avenue or downloaded.

SMILE AT FIONA AND OTHER BABIES
AT THE CINCINNATI ZOO

Babies make us smile, and no place in town evokes more happy smiles than the Cincinnati Zoo and Botanical Gardens during its annual May celebration of "Zoo Babies." It's renowned for protecting and propagating endangered species including Western lowland gorillas (50 have been born here), as well as elephants, cheetahs, tigers, giraffes, and especially Fiona, a prematurely born Nile hippopotamus, who arrived in 2017 and grew quickly to viral media stardom. (She weighed 26 pounds at birth; by age 2 she was close to 1,000 pounds.) As of 2022, Fiona has a baby brother, Fritz. The zoo opened in 1875, making it America's second oldest. It has more than 500 animal species in natural habitats across a gorgeously landscaped 75-acre campus with more than 3,000 different plants. The Zoo's Festival of Lights, a Cincinnati holiday tradition was voted by *USA Today* as the best in the nation.

3400 Vine St., 513-281-4700
cincinnatizoo.org

THROW YOUR VOICE AROUND
AT VENT HAVEN MUSEUM

You don't have to be a dummy to visit this unique museum with more than 800 ventriloquist figures from 20 countries. Stop by and you'll see a lot of familiar faces, from Bea Arthur to Ronald Reagan, as well as a photo of Johnny Carson with his sons and a dummy he told them was their brother. Vent Haven began in the 1930s, the passion of William Shakespeare Berger, a Cincinnati businessman. (He passed away in 1973, but Vent Haven lives on.) The museum, five miles south of Downtown Cincinnati, is open seasonally between May 1 and September 30. Admission and 45- to 90-minute tours by appointment only. Vent Haven hosts an annual international conVENTion, attended by hundreds of ventriloquists. Do their lips move?

33 W Maple Ave., Ft. Mitchell, KY, 859-341-0461
venthavenmuseum.com

SPARK AN INTEREST IN FIREFIGHTING
AT THE FIRE MUSEUM

In 1853, before any other American city stepped up to professionalize firefighting, Cincinnati established the first full-time, paid, professional fire department. The Cincinnati Fire Museum is housed in a Renaissance Revival firehouse built in 1906 that's now on the National Register of Historic Places. It was a station for Engine Company #45 until 1960. Today, historical displays and numerous artifacts of firefighting are displayed, including leather buckets and a fire-alarm drum (used to alert Cincinnatians to dangerous urban fires early in the 19th century) and an Ahrens steam pumper from 1884. Educational exhibits about fire safety and what it takes to be a firefighter make it a great destination for school trips, retirement communities, and more.

315 W Court St., #1, 513-621-5553
cincyfiremuseum.com

EXPERIENCE SCULPTURE IN THE GREAT OUTDOORS
AT PYRAMID HILL

Oversized sculptures are typically the stuff of museums, city plazas, or historical destinations, but Pyramid Hill Sculpture Park and Museum is a 265-acre sculpture park in a rural setting where you can see more than 50 monumental works thoughtfully placed in natural outdoor locations. It's a beautiful, serene place to visit for a drive in your car or via "Art Cart" (aka golf carts available for rental). You can also walk from site to site around the grounds. The park is also home to the Ancient Sculpture Museum, with a collection of Greek, Roman, Etruscan, and Egyptian sculptures dating to 1550 BC and featuring an Egyptian sarcophagus, terra cotta sculptures, and ancient coins. A smaller gallery features local and regional artists in rotating monthly exhibitions.

1763 Hamilton-Cleves Rd., Hamilton, 513-868-8336
pyramidhill.org

SEE WHERE
HARRIET BEECHER STOWE
BEGAN *UNCLE TOM'S CABIN*

Harriet Beecher Stowe wrote *Uncle Tom's Cabin* (1852) after living in Cincinnati and seeing the injustices of slavery. She came here at the age of 21 when her father, the fiery preacher Rev. Lyman Beecher, was named president of the Lane Theological Seminary. From 1832 to 1850, her life in Cincinnati shaped her attitudes and inspired her to write her best-selling novel, a singular catalyst for the abolition movement. When she met President Abraham Lincoln a decade after *Uncle Tom's Cabin* was published, he is said to have exclaimed, "So you are the little woman who wrote the book that started this great war!" The home where the Beechers lived in Walnut Hills still stands, today a museum of her life and her commitment to the civil and human rights movements.

Harriet Beecher Stowe House
2950 Gilbert Ave., 513-751-0651
stowehousecincy.org

VISIT RIPLEY
AND LEARN ABOUT THE
UNDERGROUND RAILROAD

The small Ohio River town of Ripley (50 miles east of Cincinnati in Brown County) has a big history. Early in the 19th century, it was a significant crossing point for people escaping slavery through the Underground Railroad. Many prominent abolitionists lived in Ripley, including John Rankin, who in 1822 built a house on Liberty Hill overlooking the town from which he could signal escaping slaves with a lantern on a flagpole. The John Rankin House is still there, now a National Historic Landmark. Margaret Garner escaped across the frozen Ohio in 1838; her plight inspired the character of Eliza in Harriet Beecher Stowe's *Uncle Tom's Cabin*, the best-selling book of the 19th century. Don't miss the John P. Parker House, the home of a freed slave and inventor who helped hundreds of people on their way to freedom.

John Rankin House
6152 Rankin Hill Rd., Ripley, 937-392-4044

John P. Parker Historical Society
300 N Front St., Ripley, 937-392-4188
johnparkerhouse.org

VISIT THE TROPICS
AT KROHN CONSERVATORY

Cincinnati winters can be bone chilling, but if you need a reminder of warmer climes, you should swing by Krohn Conservatory in Eden Park. Built in 1933 at the height of the Art Deco era, it's a gigantic greenhouse with a rainforest waterfall and exotic plants, including palms, tropical and desert environments, as well as special areas for orchids and bonsai. Krohn changes through the year, thanks to special exhibits. A favorite is the annual springtime Butterfly Show, where thousands of butterflies are airborne in a showroom inside a specially themed garden. For the holidays there are poinsettias with model trains that circle detailed recreations of iconic Cincinnati buildings, made from natural materials.

1501 Eden Park Dr., 513-421-4086
cincinnatiparks.com/krohn-conservatory

REFLECT ON STAINED GLASS
AT THE CATHEDRAL BASILICA

St. Mary's Cathedral Basilica of the Assumption in Covington opened in 1895; the Roman Catholic Gothic-styled structure was elevated to the rank of "minor basilica" in 1953. Its interior was modeled after the Abbey Church of St. Denis in Paris, with murals by renowned painter Frank Duveneck. The building's most gorgeous features are its 82 stained glass windows, made in Munich, Germany, and installed in 1910. The north transept's beautiful handmade stained glass window at 67 feet high and 24 feet wide is said to be the world's largest. It depicts the fifth-century council that proclaimed Mary as Mother of God. Two massive rose windows, 26 feet in diameter, are also spectacular. Visitors are welcome during regular open hours, Monday–Saturday, 10 a.m.–4 p.m. Hour-long guided tours can be arranged in advance.

1130 Madison Ave., Covington, KY, 859-431-2060
covcathedral.com

TIP
The historic Cincinnati May Festival
presents one of its annual choral concerts at the
Cathedral Basilica, showing off its gorgeous
acoustics as well as the beautiful interior.

VISIT MUSEUMS
IN A HISTORIC TRAIN STATION

Cincinnati Union Terminal opened in 1933. During World War II it welcomed 216 trains daily, serving 17,000 passengers. Its Art Deco architecture features a half-domed rotunda (largest in the Western Hemisphere), 180 feet across and 106 feet high with mosaics depicting Cincinnati's history and the opening of the American West. In 1990, it became the Cincinnati Museum Center, home to the Cincinnati Museum of Natural History & Science (with a Dinosaur Hall featuring a 35-foot-long skeleton), Cincinnati History Museum (with a recreation of Cincinnati's Public Landing in 1850), the Children's Museum, and an Omnimax Theater with a five-story, domed screen. A recent $228 million renovation has preserved and enhanced the 500,000-square-foot building. The recently added Holocaust and Humanity Center commemorates the numerous Holocaust survivors who arrived at the train station to rebuild their lives. The Museum Center presents blockbuster exhibitions and special shows (including model trains for the holidays), attracting visitors from near and far, with attendance of nearly 1.5 million annually.

1301 Western Ave., 513-287-7000
cincymuseum.org

DROP IN
ON A HISTORIC TAFT FAMILY HOME FOR FINE ART

One of Cincinnati's oldest homes also happens to be one of the finest art museums in America: the Taft Museum of Art was built as a private residence in 1820. From 1873 to 1929, avid art collectors Charles and Anna Taft lived there. Charles's half-brother, William Howard Taft, accepted his presidential nomination on the portico in 1908. In 1927, Charles and Anna deeded their home and their art holdings to the people of Cincinnati—paintings (including a Rembrandt, a Whistler, and a Turner), Chinese porcelains, Limoges enamels, watches, sculptures, and furniture. The Taft has added exhibition space, a lecture hall, a shop, and a café, built around a lovely formal garden. The building's original entryway features landscape murals painted by Robert S. Duncanson (1821–1872), an important African American artist. To mark the building's 200th anniversary, the historic house underwent extensive historic preservation.

Lytle Park, Downtown, 316 Pike St., 513-241-0343
taftmuseum.org

GET SHAKIN'
AT THE OTTO M. BUDIG THEATER

Since the 1990s, Cincinnati Shakespeare Company has presented engaging productions of Shakespeare's plays and works by other renowned playwrights, ranging from Oscar Wilde to August Wilson, as well as stage adaptations of classic novels and movies. In its first two decades, it staged the complete "canon," all 38 of the Bard's plays, a feat achieved by just a few theaters around the world. In 2017, it moved into a modern facility on the Elm Street "arts corridor" in Over-the-Rhine with 244 seats, all within 20 feet of the state-of-the-art stage. Productions are performed by professional actors who can be serious or silly, just as Shakespeare's company at London's Globe Theatre did four centuries ago. Shows are typically family-friendly and approachable, especially entertaining for young audiences.

1195 Elm St., Over-the-Rhine, 513-381-2273
cincyshakes.com

TIP

During July and August, Cincy Shakes tours several outdoor productions to dozens of parks around the Tristate. "Free Shakespeare in the Park" offers abridged, portable shows, usually performed by a half-dozen actors taking on several roles apiece. It's a fine way to give kids a taste of live theater.

PRAY THE IMMACULATA STEPS
ON GOOD FRIDAY

Cincinnati supposedly has seven hills, but if you ask for the list, you'll get more. Regardless, this is a hilly town. People in the 19th century built steps to get around. Many are still here, and one has a renowned tradition. The Church of the Immaculata in Mt. Adams is at the top of a flight of 85 steps. Since 1860, thousands of faithful Roman Catholics have climbed them to the church's front door annually between midnight on Holy Thursday and midnight on Good Friday, praying the Rosary on each step. It's the only pilgrimage of its kind in the world, attracting from 8,000 to 10,000 people most years. Pick your starting point: the upper steps start on St. Gregory Street just below the church; the middle steps begin on Columbia Parkway; the lower steps take off from Adams Crossing.

30 Guido St., 513-721-6544
hcparish.org

WALK ACROSS THE OHIO RIVER
ON THE ROEBLING SUSPENSION BRIDGE

On December 1, 1866, 166,000 people walked across the bridge between Cincinnati and Covington, Kentucky, for the first time. At 1,057 feet, it was the longest suspension bridge in the world. It's named for engineer John A. Roebling, who learned from this project what he needed to know to design and build the much larger (and world-famous) Brooklyn Bridge, completed in 1883. His Cincinnati bridge was begun in 1856 but stalled for a decade due to a shortage of funds and the American Civil War. It continues to be a frequent connector across the Ohio River for cars, buses, and pedestrians. Look for three plaques with QR codes for brief video tours of "The Anchor House," "Towers," and "Mid Span."

roeblingbridge.org

TIP
Just beyond the Roebling Bridge's southern terminus, you'll find Roebling Point Books & Coffee (306 Greenup St., Covington), a charming independent bookseller and coffee shop, featuring books about local history, great coffee, and an environment that's dog friendly.

REVEL IN
A PALACE OF ART DECO
AT THE CAREW TOWER

The Carew Tower is a 49-story building completed in 1931 in the heart of Downtown Cincinnati. It's the city's second-tallest building, but it has the most iconic presence of any structure Downtown. Thanks to its gorgeous French Art Deco style, it was added to the National Register of Historic Places in 1994. The complex predates New York City's Rockefeller Center (1931–1939), designed on a similar concept, combining offices, shops, restaurants, and a glamorous hotel. The Hilton Cincinnati Netherland Plaza and its glorious Hall of Mirrors were inspired by the Palace of Versailles. Winston Churchill, Elvis Presley, Eleanor Roosevelt, Bing Crosby, and John and Jackie Kennedy were past guests. Some mind-boggling stats about the Carew complex: 15,000 tons of structural steel were needed to build its skeleton, and four million bricks were used for its outer structure. The building has 8,000 windows, all affording great views.

Carew Tower Arcade
441 Vine St.

Hilton Cincinnati Netherland Plaza
35 W 5th St., 513-421-9100
cincinnatinetherlandplaza.hilton.com

TIP

From the Carew Tower's Observation Deck, you get a 360-degree view of the region. Bring a few quarters to use the binocular viewers and get a clear picture no matter which way you point them—25 cents per view.

SEE THE NEWEST ART
AT THE CONTEMPORARY ARTS CENTER

Cincinnati's Contemporary Arts Center has been offering seriously creative works since its founding in 1939 by three women who formed the Modern Art Society, establishing one of the very first contemporary arts institutions in the United States. It has no collection of its own, preferring to mount exhibitions of photography, sculpture, painting, architecture, performance art, and new media reflecting "the art of the last five minutes." In 1990, an exhibition of controversial photos by Robert Mapplethorpe led to criminal charges against the CAC's director; he was acquitted in a trial that drew national attention. The CAC's home since 2003 is the Lois and Richard Rosenthal Center for Contemporary Art, a work of art itself, a jigsaw puzzle of slightly askew stacked blocks designed by renowned architect Zaha Hadid, the first woman to design a major museum in the United States.

44 E 6th St., 513-345-8400
contemporaryartscenter.org

TUNNEL INTO LOCAL HISTORY
ON AN AMERICAN LEGACY TOUR

Beneath Downtown Cincinnati at a depth of 45 feet or so is a network of tunnels created in the 19th century by the city's flourishing brewers. In these chilly passages, beer could be fermented and cooled, as well as delivered to the 130 or so saloons, bars, beer gardens, and theaters in the Over-the-Rhine neighborhood. You can visit these bygone catacombs, thanks to a "Queen City Underground" trek by American Legacy Tours. Led by knowledgeable guides (several are high school history teachers), these tours are educational, entertaining, and extremely popular. Once you've seen the depths of OTR, check out the company's other adventures, looking for ghosts, bootleggers, or gangsters in OTR and across the Ohio River in Covington and Newport.

1332 Vine St., 859-951-8560
americanlegacytours.com

GAZE AT MURALS
ON WALLS ALL OVER TOWN

Outdoor murals can be found in dozens of neighborhoods throughout Cincinnati and Northern Kentucky thanks to ArtWorks, an award-winning nonprofit that trains and employs local teenagers with artistic skills to create public art on a grand scale. The kids get paying summer jobs plus experience managed by professional artists. They've created more than 200 murals with subjects that are historic, imaginative, or fanciful: "Martha, The Last Carrier Pigeon (1914)" replicates naturalist artist John Ruthven's sweeping portrait of the final survivor of an extinct species (she lived out her final days at the Cincinnati Zoo). "The Hands That Built Our City" displays images of workers' hands from mosaics that once graced the interior of Union Terminal. Iconic local characters are popular—boxer Ezzard Charles and rock-and-roller James Brown to astronaut Neil Armstrong. Check out walking tours—self-guided or with knowledgeable volunteers—on the website.

2460 Gilbert Ave., Walnut Hills, 513-333-0388
artworkscincinnati.org

TIP

On Covington's floodwall, adjacent to the Roebling Suspension Bridge, is a striking collection of 18 panels depicting the city's history. Painted a few sections at a time between 2002 and 2009 by a team of artists led by renowned muralist Robert Dafford, they chronicle everything from ancient buffalo roads to bridges to German heritage.

Riverside Dr., Covington
covington.gov/forms-documents/view/
roebling-murals-at-the-covington-riverfront

VISIT THE BIRTHPLACE
OF AMERICA'S 27TH PRESIDENT

In the 19th century, Mt. Auburn was Cincinnati's first suburb, on a ridge above the crowded, polluted city. Sedate homes lined Auburn Avenue, including the birthplace of William Howard Taft, America's 27th president (1909–1913) and 10th Chief Justice of the Supreme Court (1921–1930). In 1857, Taft was born in a room on the first floor of the house (owned by his parents from 1851 to 1889), and he lived in the 1840s house until he left for Yale University in 1874. Today, the national historic site has an education center adjacent to the historic house, outfitted with period furniture in four rooms on the first floor. It has been restored to look as it did during Taft's childhood, with family portraits and books owned by the Tafts. The second floor offers exhibits about Taft's public life.

William Howard Taft Birthplace
2038 Auburn Ave., 513-684-3262
nps.gov/wiho

RING IN SOME PEACE
WITH A GIGANTIC BELL

The World Peace Bell in Newport is one of the world's largest free-swinging bells. It weighs 33 tons; the clapper alone is almost four tons. It was cast in France in 1998, overseen by Cincinnati's historic Verdin Bell Company. It was shipped across the Atlantic Ocean and up the Mississippi and Ohio rivers in time for its dedication on December 31, 1999, marking the transition to a new millennium with a peal that resounded for 25 miles. Originally envisioned to top off an 85-bell, 1,400-foot-tall carillon, it's the sole survivor of a project that never gained the necessary financing. Nevertheless, this magnificent bell, suspended in a striking glass enclosure, is intended as a symbol of freedom and peace. It is rung daily at 11:55 a.m.

425 York St., Newport, KY, 859-655-7700
southbankpartners.com/world-peace-bell/what-is-t.aspx

LEARN MORE
ABOUT CINCINNATI'S
JEWISH HERITAGE

The first Jewish community west of the Allegheny Mountains was in Cincinnati. Isaac M. Wise, who founded American Reform Judaism and Hebrew Union College, was a prominent rabbi here. Mayerson Hall on HUC's Cincinnati campus is home to the Skirball Museum, established in 1913, one of the oldest repositories of Jewish cultural artifacts in America. The Skirball's core exhibit, *An Eternal People: The Jewish Experience*, portrays the cultural, historical, and religious heritage of the Jewish people. Holdings of Jewish artifacts and memorabilia tripled in 2015 with the massive donation of the B'nai B'rith Klutznick Collection of artistic and cultural heritage, everything from a figurine of legendary baseball pitcher Sandy Koufax to etchings by Rembrandt.

Skirball Museum, Hebrew Union College
3101 Clifton Ave.
huc.edu/research/museums/skirball-museum-cincinnati

TIP

The Plum Street Temple (1866), officially named in honor of Rabbi Isaac M. Wise, is one of the oldest synagogues in the United States. Its architecture with minarets is unusual for a synagogue; it was inspired by the 12th-century Jewish philosopher Maimonides, born in Moorish Spain. The original flooring, chandeliers, candelabras, wall stenciling, pews, and pulpit furnishings are intact. Tours are available on Thursday mornings; call in advance.

720 Plum St., 513-739-2556
wisetemple.org

MEET A TWO-HEADED CALF
AT THE BEHRINGER-CRAWFORD MUSEUM

The Behringer-Crawford Museum began in 1950 based on William Behringer's collection of natural history curiosities, especially a taxidermied "two-headed calf." (Rather than one body with two heads, it's actually conjoined twins, two attached bodies.) The oddity inspired an annual "Two-Headed Calf Community Service Award," recognizing Northern Kentuckians who have contributed to the preservation and celebration of regional history, art, and culture. The regional museum is a family-friendly place, especially during the holidays when a toy train exhibit takes over, a popular attraction for more than a quarter-century. Located in the historic 19th-century Devou family home, the museum is the centerpiece of Covington's Devou Park.

1600 Montague Rd., Covington, KY, 859-491-4003
bcmuseum.org

COMPARE AND CONTRAST SCIENCE VS. RELIGION
IN KENTUCKY'S BOONE COUNTY

In Northern Kentucky's Boone County, you can explore the extremes of evolution philosophy. At Big Bone Lick State Historic Site in Union, you'll find displays about Ice Age mammals, geology from 400-plus million years in the past, and the chronology of science. Just 12 miles to the northwest in Petersburg, you'll find a very different perspective at the Creation Museum, a religiously themed institution that brings pages of the Bible to life and explains the origins of the universe based on a literal interpretation of the Book of Genesis. Exhibits portray Earth as being 6,000 years old and put early humans in the same era as the dinosaurs. Science or religion? It's your choice.

Creation Museum
2800 Bullittsburgh Church Rd., Petersburg, KY, 800-721-2298
creationmuseum.org

Big Bone Lick State Historic Site
330 Beaver Rd., Union, KY, 859-384-4267
parks.ky.gov/parks/historicsites/big-bone-lick

MARCH WITH YOUR NEIGHBORS
IN THE REDS OPENING DAY PARADE

Cincinnatians love parades. The year's biggest is the annual Findlay Market Parade on Reds Opening Day. Because the Reds were baseball's first professional team in 1869, they have the privilege of opening every season at home. The day is marked as a local holiday: kids skip school, office workers call in sick, and Race and Fifth Streets between Findlay Market and the ballpark on the Riverfront are lined four and five deep with fans dressed in red. The parade, typically two hours long starting at noon, features marching bands, fire engines, horse-drawn wagons (often including the Budweiser Clydesdales), drill teams, sports celebs, and lots of baseball-themed, homemade floats. It's a celebration of hope, regardless of the team's prospects, and everybody's a fan.

findlaymarketparade.com

TIP

The bohemian neighborhood of Northside lays claim to the "best damn parade in Cincinnati" every Fourth of July. The zany stream of humanity features clowns, dogs, and people dressed outlandishly, unicycles, hula hoops, skate boards, lawnmower drill teams, crazy floats, politicians (of course), and lots of candy for the onlookers. The very tongue-in-cheek throng marches down the Hamilton Avenue hill to a Rock 'n' Roll Carnival in Hoffner Park. (Look for this parade on Facebook.)

SHOPPING
AND FASHION

BUY HISTORIC CERAMIC ART
AT ROOKWOOD POTTERY

In 1876, Maria Longworth, a Cincinnati native, was dazzled by a ceramic art exhibition in Philadelphia. In 1880, she established a pottery studio in Cincinnati: Rookwood Pottery was the first female-owned and managed manufacturing company in the United States. She hired artists, especially women, and encouraged creativity and new techniques that won international recognition for gorgeous glazes and elegant designs as well as architectural items, such as fireplace tiles. (The Cincinnati Art Museum has a gallery dedicated to Rookwood items.) The company was dormant for much of the 20th century, but it's back to life now with new kilns and artists, reproducing gorgeous items from the past and creating beautiful new tiles, award trophies, and other ceramic creations.

1920 Race St., Over-the-Rhine, 513-281-2004 (800-537-1605)
rookwood.com

TIP

You can tour Rookwood's production studio near Findlay Market, see the artists designing new items and artisans manufacturing historic, collectible, and decorative works. Many items are available for purchase, and there's a showroom displaying a wide array of tile treatments.

1209 Jackson St., 513-579-1209

EXPLORE SIX ACRES OF GROCERIES
AT JUNGLE JIM'S

More than 80,000 shoppers visit Jungle Jim's International Market locations weekly, browsing more than 180,000 products from around the world across 300,000 square feet of shopping space in suburban Cincinnati. Purchase items for Asian fare (more than 10 countries are represented) or genuine Indian products (rice, tea, spices), as well as supplies for Hispanic, European, Eastern European, Middle Eastern, and African cuisines. The brainchild of antic entrepreneur Jim Bonaminio, Jungle Jim's has been an area attraction since 1971, not just for shopping but for food demonstrations, a cooking school, and special festivals for cheese, beer, and wine.

5440 Dixie Hwy., Fairfield
4450 Eastgate S Dr., Union Township, 513-674-6000
junglejims.com

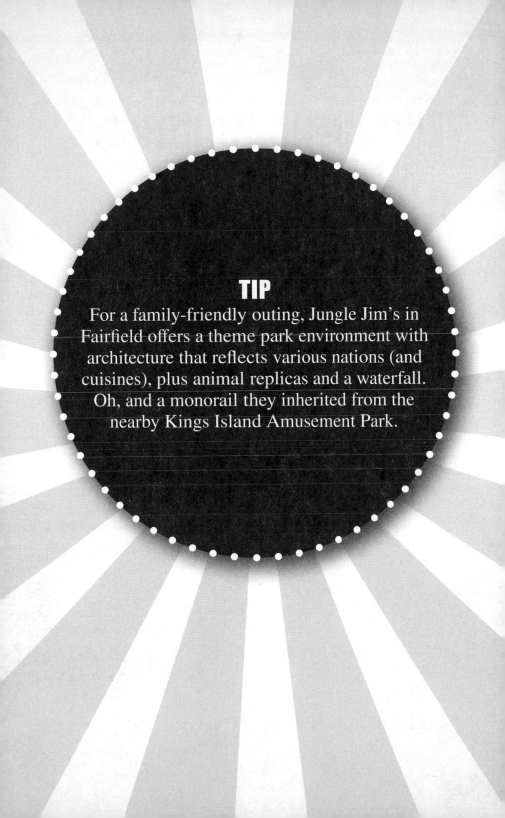

TIP

For a family-friendly outing, Jungle Jim's in Fairfield offers a theme park environment with architecture that reflects various nations (and cuisines), plus animal replicas and a waterfall. Oh, and a monorail they inherited from the nearby Kings Island Amusement Park.

EXPERIENCE DIVERSITY
AT HISTORIC FINDLAY MARKET

Once upon a time Cincinnatians could shop at nine different markets. Findlay Market, founded in 1852, is the sole survivor, today Ohio's oldest continuously operated public market. It's a quintessential urban shopping experience, especially dense on Saturday mornings, with people stocking up on meat, fish, poultry, produce, flowers, cheese, deli, and ethnic foods. But you'll find more than shopping: It's a socially, economically, racially, and ethnically diverse intersection of people from all over the city—flavored by musicians, gift vendors, politicians, and more. Hang out at the beer garden, buy ready-to-eat items, or stock up with groceries. It's all about wandering and savoring and running into friends and neighbors.

1801 Race St., Over-the-Rhine
findlaymarket.org

TIPS

Stop by Colonel De Gourmet Herbs & Spices (colonelde.com) and explore the mind-boggling array of spices, seasonings, rubs, sugars, and flavors. The staff can advise you about the best spice for that pork roast or the perfect seasoning for the fresh salmon you just bought. More great choices: Blue Oven Bakery; LK at Findlay (handmade smoked sausages); Dojo Gelato; Eckerlin Meats; Eli's BBQ; J. E. Gibbs Cheese and Sausage; Greekish; Luken's Poultry, Fish & Seafood; and SKT Pottery. Just across the sidewalk from the market, don't miss Madison's, a small grocery offering local, organic, and nutritious items, plus a wide selection of bulk beans, rice, nuts, flours, and grains.

GET COOKING
WITH ARTICHOKE CURATED COOKWARE

Once you've finished shopping for produce, meats, spices, and more at Findlay Market, walk a few steps north on Elm Street to Artichoke, a "curated cookware" shop, designed to meet the needs of experienced and novice cooks. Need a special pot or prep tool? The staff is ready to provide personal advice—maybe even suggesting two or three options. They cover all the basics in cookware and bakeware, and they are always on the lookout for visionary, imaginatively designed appliances, kitchen cutlery, and other tools. The store features a small kitchen area to demonstrate devices and offer cooking and food prep classes on topics ranging from cocktails to pressure cookers. They'll also sharpen your knives for $5 per blade.

1825 Elm St., Findlay Market, Over-the-Rhine, 513-263-1002
artichokeotr.com

FIND A GEM IN THE QUEEN CITY
AT RICHTER & PHILLIPS JEWELERS

In 1896, Edward Richter and three Phillips brothers opened a jewelry store in downtown Cincinnati. They also produced a mail-order catalog for customers nationwide. Frederick W. Fehr, a diamond salesman, bought out the owners in 1930 and ran the store for 42 years, until he was 90. Fehr's son and grandsons have continued the tradition of selling beautiful jewelry and watches from a sparkling downtown location at the corner of Sixth and Main streets, a one-time bank building with a basement vault and space for an entertainment venue. Getting married or need a watch battery? This is the best destination.

601 Main St., Downtown
richterphillips.com

FIND YOUR FAVORITE ANIMAL ON HANDCRAFTED POTTERY
AT SKT CERAMICS

This porcelain pottery and illustration studio was launched in Brooklyn, New York, in 2009 by Cincinnatian Susannah Tisue. In 2017, she brought her operation back to her hometown, first with a stand at Findlay Market and now in a design workshop and showroom in a renovated 1910 vaudeville theater building in Walnut Hills that once held a 300-seat theater. Tisue leads a team of skilled artists who produce high-fired durable tableware, printed textiles, and gifts featuring her delicate illustrations of animals and Cincinnati scenes. Her one-of-a-kind designs are cherished by knowledgeable lovers of ceramics.

SKT Ceramics at Century Design Workshop
2449 Gilbert Ave., Walnut Hills, 513-376-6183
sktceramics.com

SKT Ceramics at Findlay Market
1801 Race St., Over-the-Rhine

TIP

Upstairs at SKT Ceramics you'll find cabinetmaker Michael Miritello, who happens to be Tisue's husband. His Century Design Workshop designs, builds, and repairs furniture and cabinetry for residential and commercial spaces, using sustainably sourced wood and traditional joinery techniques. Tisue and Miritello incorporate their fine art training into their work, and they are committed to the creation of well-made, carefully considered objects.

centurydesignworkshop.com

MEET ARTISTS AND BUY THEIR WORKS
AT PENDLETON ART CENTER

You don't have to be an art connoisseur to check out the Pendleton Art Center, the world's largest collection of artists under one roof. On the Final Friday evening (6–10 p.m.) of each month, you can browse a honeycomb of galleries spread across eight floors of a 1909 shoe factory and warehouse with the original pine floors and arched windows, eight feet tall. The Pendleton is now where more than 200 artists get creative on a regular basis with painting, crafts, sculpture, metalwork, jewelry, photography, and more. If you're serious about building a local art collection, this is the place to start. If you see things you like, you can come back on the Saturday after Final Friday (11 a.m.–3 p.m.) for "Art in Action," a chance to hear lectures, meet the artists, and view and purchase their artwork.

1310 Pendleton St., 513-559-3958
pendletonartcenter.com

TIP

Take the elevator to the eighth floor (it's a rickety old freight job, but it will get you there) and work your way down. It's tough to see all eight floors in one four-hour evening, so plan to come back another Final Friday.

GET FIRED UP
AT BROMWELL'S

The oldest business in Cincinnati began in 1819. Over the course of nearly two centuries, it's been owned and managed by just three families. At Bromwell's Downtown studio store, you'll find top-quality fireplaces and accessories as well as distinctive home furnishings and gifts. They're the go-to place to find fireplace inserts, gas and electric logs, outdoor fireplaces and grills, furniture, lighting, mantles and mantle shelves, wall décor, and art. Everything is on display in settings that help you imagine the total picture. Even in the 21st century, the hearth is the center of most homes. Bromwell's can help you create one that's eye-catching and distinctively yours.

117 W 4th St., Downtown, 513-621-0620
bromwells.com

PUT A LID ON IT
AT BATSAKES HAT SHOP

Gus Miller was 17 when he arrived in Cincinnati from Greece to work in his uncle's hat shop. He swept floors at first, but before long he learned about making hats. He's still at it today, and his clients have included opera star Luciano Pavarotti, presidents (Reagan, Bush, and Bush), Bengals owner and coach Paul Brown, and singers from Tony Bennett to Bob Dylan. Batsakes isn't just a place where hats are sold: they're made by hand on-site, tailored for individuals. Customers—local, national, and international—come back again and again. Once you've found the perfect hat, sit in one of the six seats on the shoeshine stand and be polished—from head to toe.

1 W 6th St., Downtown, 513-721-9345

FIND THE PERFECT WEDDING GOWN (AND MORE)
IN THE READING BRIDAL DISTRICT

Planning a wedding? In the quiet Cincinnati suburb of Reading, you can shop till you drop in North America's largest bridal district, featuring more than 44 wedding-related businesses and services along a two-mile stretch of West Benson Street. The Reading Bridal District features more than 10 gown stores with a total inventory of 9,000 wedding dresses and 2,500 choices for bridesmaids. Other vendors in the neighborhood include tux rentals, photographers, florists, bakers, makeup artists, caterers and event planners, invitation printers, music, and entertainment services. Visit the district and you'll find yourself in the company of brides-to-be, bridesmaids, and mothers from all over the Midwest!

Reading Bridal District
Between 11 and 339 W Benson St.
(Reading Road and Church Street), Reading
readingbridaldistrict.com

RIDE THE STREETCAR
AND SHOP THE CITY

Since 2016, Cincinnati has been moving people around the urban core on a modern streetcar, the Connector. It travels a 3.6-mile loop from the riverfront to the north end of Over-the-Rhine. It's a perfect way to shop the city without having to drive around or find parking, and it's free. There are 18 stops, with cars passing by every 15 minutes or so. Hop off at Fifth and Walnut for ice cream from Graeter's on Fountain Square, at Fourth and Main for Richter & Phillips Jewelers, or 12th and Vine for boutique shopping (and dining) in Over-the-Rhine. There are stops on the east and west ends of Findlay Market, too, making it easy to take advantage of the many vendors and the summertime farmers market there.

513-765-1212
cincinnati-oh.gov/streetcar

Cincinnati Streetcar

SUGGESTED
ITINERARIES

RIDE THE NO. 1 BUS

Queen City Metro Bus Route No. 1 follows an "arts & culture" route from the Cincinnati Museum Center, past the School for Creative and Performing Arts in Over-the-Rhine, to Downtown's Duke Energy Convention Center and Cincinnati City Hall, and Fountain Square then up to Mt. Adams near the Cincinnati Playhouse and the Cincinnati Art Museum, through Eden Park and past Krohn Conservatory. You can purchase a day pass for $4 and ride all day long. (You can buy it on the bus or at the Metro Sales office, 120 East 4th Street, Downtown, across from Government Square.)

Visit the Tropics at Krohn Conservatory, 93

Get Dramatic at the Cincinnati Playhouse in the Park, 82

Explore Cincinnati's Historic Creativity at the Cincinnati Art Museum, 84

Enjoy Opera or a Symphony Concert at Cincinnati Music Hall, 50

Drop In on a Historic Taft Family Home for Fine Art, 97

Wet Your Whistle at Fountain Square, 83

Visit Museums in a Historic Train Station, 96

CLASSIC CINCINNATI

Have a Three-Way in a Cincinnati Chili Parlor, 2

Revel in a Palace of Art Deco at the Carew Tower, 102

Belly Up to Cincinnati's Oldest Bar, 4

Cheer for the Musketeers or the Bearcats at the Crosstown Shootout, 77

Get Some Goetta, 5

Take In the View with Your Favorite Date at Primavista, 28

• •

FAMILY-FRIENDLY—KID STUFF

• •

BOTTOMS UP

HISTORICAL DESTINATIONS

FOOD FANTASIES

SHOPAHOLICS

• •

SPORTS

OUTDOORS

• •

CREATIVE CHOICES

ACTIVITIES
BY SEASON

• •

FALL

• •

WINTER

● ●

INDEX

● ●